Implementing AI in Business:

A Comprehensive Guide

All the texts contained in this book have been produced by OpenAI's Artificial Intelligence (AI) chat interface ChatGPT, prompted, commented, and edited by the author.

Automated responses were transferred mostly unedited as they were produced by the AI, using brackets to mark down where a relevant edit has been made, so the reader can get the most accurate impression of the automation's capabilities and limitations.

This document pretends to serve as a reference and starting point for a business transformation journey into AI assimilation. It also provides a practical exercise on how AI can be guided to provide value in a business context.

PROMPT - Let's write a comprehensive book about implementing Ai in business
RESPONSE - Certainly! Here's a comprehensive outline for a book on implementing AI in business:

Title: *Implementing AI in Business: A Comprehensive Guide*

Introduction

- **Why AI Matters**: Importance of AI in modern business.
- **Scope of the Book**: What will be covered.
- **Target Audience**: Who this book is for.

Chapter 1: Understanding AI

- **What is AI?**: Definitions and history.
- **Types of AI**: Narrow AI vs. General AI.
- **Key Concepts**: Machine learning, deep learning, neural networks.

Chapter 2: The Business Case for AI

- **Benefits of AI**: Efficiency, innovation, decision-making.
- **AI in Different Sectors**: Finance, healthcare, retail, manufacturing.
- **Case Studies**: Successful AI implementations.

Chapter 3: Preparing for AI

- **Assessing Readiness**: Evaluating current capabilities.
- **Setting Goals**: Defining objectives for AI implementation.

- **Building a Team**: Roles and responsibilities (data scientists, engineers, etc.).
- **Developing a roadmap**: Milestones, timelines and resource allocations.

Chapter 4: Data Management

- **Importance of Data**: The foundation of AI.
- **Data Collection**: Methods and best practices.
- **Data Quality**: Ensuring accuracy and relevance.
- **Data Governance**: Policies and compliance.

Chapter 5: Choosing the Right AI Solutions

- **Types of AI Technologies**: Natural language processing, computer vision, predictive analytics.
- **Build vs. Buy**: Pros and cons of in-house development vs. third-party solutions.
- **Evaluating Vendors**: Criteria for selecting AI providers.

Chapter 6: Developing AI Models

- **Machine Learning Basics**: Supervised, unsupervised, and reinforcement learning.
- **Model Training**: Data preparation, training, validation, and testing.
- **Tools and Frameworks**: TensorFlow, PyTorch, Scikit-Learn, etc.

Chapter 7: Integration and Deployment

- **System Integration**: Embedding AI into existing systems.
- **Deployment Strategies**: On-premise vs. cloud, hybrid solutions.
- **Monitoring and Maintenance**: Ensuring ongoing performance and improvements.

Chapter 8: Ethical and Legal Considerations

- **AI Ethics**: Bias, transparency, accountability.
- **Regulatory Compliance**: GDPR, CCPA, and other regulations.
- **Corporate Responsibility**: Ensuring ethical use of AI.

Chapter 9: Managing Change

- **Change Management**: Strategies for smooth transitions.
- **Training and Support**: Educating staff and stakeholders.
- **Measuring Success**: KPIs and metrics for AI projects.

Chapter 10: Future Trends in AI

- **Emerging Technologies**: Quantum computing, edge AI.
- **AI and Society**: Impact on jobs, economy, and culture.
- **Preparing for the Future**: Staying ahead in the AI landscape.

Conclusion

- **Recap**: Summarizing key points.
- **Final Thoughts**: Encouragement for ongoing learning and adaptation.

Appendices

- **Glossary of Terms**: Definitions of common AI terminology.
- **Resources**: Books, courses, and websites for further learning.
- **Templates and Checklists**: Practical tools for AI implementation.

[...]

This outline provides a comprehensive structure for a book on implementing AI in business. Each chapter can be expanded with detailed content, examples, and practical advice to guide businesses through the entire process of adopting AI technologies.

PROMPT - Write a thoughtful and thorough introduction for this book, abounding on why AI Matters and Importance of AI in modern business, the scope of the book and what will be covered, and lastly the targeted audience and who this book is intended for. Avoid summarizing, keep the sintaxis light and the style in prose, in the most conversational way, keeping the tone of voice professional but amicable.

Introduction

Artificial Intelligence (AI) has emerged as a powerful force, reshaping industries and revolutionizing how businesses operate. From enhancing efficiency to driving innovation, AI holds the potential to unlock new opportunities and transform the way we approach challenges in the modern business landscape. This book is a comprehensive guide designed to help you navigate the complexities of AI and harness its capabilities to drive your business forward.

[

In today's fast-paced and data-driven world, the ability to quickly adapt and make informed decisions is crucial for success. AI matters because it empowers businesses to process vast amounts of data, uncover insights, and make decisions with unprecedented speed and accuracy. It automates repetitive tasks, optimizes processes, and enhances customer experiences, allowing organizations to focus on strategic initiatives and innovation.

AI is not just a technological advancement; it's a strategic imperative. Companies that leverage AI effectively can gain a competitive edge, improve operational efficiency, and create more value for their customers. Whether it's predicting market trends, personalizing customer interactions, or automating complex processes, AI has the potential to revolutionize every aspect of business.

The importance of AI in modern business cannot be overstated. It touches every industry, from finance and healthcare to retail and manufacturing, offering solutions that were once thought to be impossible. In finance, AI helps in risk management and fraud detection. In healthcare, it improves diagnostics and personalizes treatment plans. In retail, it enhances customer experiences and optimizes supply chains. In manufacturing, it drives efficiency through predictive maintenance and quality control.

AI also plays a pivotal role in decision-making. By analyzing vast amounts of data, AI provides businesses with actionable insights, helping them make informed decisions quickly. This ability to predict outcomes and adapt to changing conditions is invaluable in a world where the pace of change is accelerating.

This book is structured to provide a thorough understanding of AI and its applications in business. Here's what you'll find within its pages:

We start with the basics, exploring definitions, history, types of AI, and key concepts like machine learning and neural networks, moving then into the benefits of AI, its applications in different sectors, and real-world case studies of successful AI implementations.

We will set you on a path to understand how to align AI initiatives with your business goals, identify opportunities, and set realistic expectations, discover the importance of data as the foundation of AI, methods for data collection, ensuring data quality, and data governance.

Explore different AI technologies, weigh the pros and cons of building vs. buying AI solutions, and learn how to evaluate vendors. Dive into machine learning basics, model training, and the tools and frameworks available for AI development.

Learn how to embed AI into existing systems, choose deployment strategies, and ensure ongoing performance through monitoring and maintenance.

We will also address AI ethics, regulatory compliance, and corporate responsibility to ensure ethical use of AI.

Get strategies for smooth transitions, training and support for staff and stakeholders, and metrics for measuring success and stay ahead by exploring emerging technologies, understanding AI's impact on society, and preparing for future advancements.

This book is intended for a diverse audience, including business leaders, managers, data scientists, and anyone interested in leveraging AI for business growth. Whether you are a CEO looking to innovate, a manager seeking to optimize operations, or a data scientist aiming to develop cutting-edge AI solutions, this book provides valuable insights and practical guidance.

For business leaders and managers, it offers strategic perspectives on aligning AI with business objectives and making informed decisions about AI investments. For data scientists and AI practitioners, it provides detailed technical insights into developing and deploying AI models, along with ethical considerations and best practices.

Our goal is to demystify AI, making it accessible and actionable for professionals across various fields. We hope to inspire you to explore the possibilities of AI, equip you with the knowledge to implement AI solutions effectively, and encourage you to continue learning and adapting in this rapidly evolving landscape.

As you embark on this journey through the world of AI, remember that the true power of AI lies not just in the technology itself, but in how it is applied to solve real-world problems and create value. We invite you to dive in, explore the chapters ahead, and unlock the transformative potential of AI for your business.
]

PROMPT - Write a comprehensive and thorough chapter 1 about Understanding AI, with subchapters on What is AI?: Definitions and history; Types of AI: Narrow AI vs. General AI ; and Key Concepts: Machine learning, deep learning, neural networks

Chapter 1: Understanding AI

Artificial Intelligence (AI) is a transformative technology that is reshaping industries, driving innovation, and offering new opportunities for businesses and society. This chapter aims to provide a comprehensive understanding of AI by exploring its definitions and history, distinguishing between different types of AI, and delving into key concepts like machine learning, deep learning, and neural networks.

1.1 What is AI?: Definitions and History

Definitions of AI

AI refers to the simulation of human intelligence in machines that are programmed to think and learn like humans. These systems can perform tasks such as visual perception, speech recognition, decision-making, and language translation. AI can be broadly defined as the capability of a machine to imitate intelligent human behavior.

The field of AI encompasses a variety of subfields, including machine learning, natural language processing, robotics, and computer vision. Each of these subfields focuses on specific aspects of intelligence, such as learning from data, understanding human language, and perceiving the environment.

History of AI

The history of AI can be traced back to ancient myths and legends about artificial beings endowed with intelligence. However, the formal field of AI research began in the mid-20th century.

- **Early Beginnings (1940s-1950s)**: The foundations of AI were laid with the development of the first electronic computers. Alan Turing, a British mathematician, proposed the concept of a "universal machine" that could simulate the logic of any computer algorithm. His famous Turing Test, introduced in 1950, became a fundamental criterion for evaluating a machine's ability to exhibit intelligent behavior.
- **The Birth of AI (1956)**: The term "Artificial Intelligence" was coined at the Dartmouth Conference in 1956, which is considered the birthplace of AI as a field of study. Researchers like John McCarthy, Marvin Minsky, Nathaniel Rochester, and Claude Shannon proposed that human intelligence could be precisely described and simulated by a machine.
- **Early Optimism (1950s-1970s)**: The early years of AI research were marked by optimism and significant progress. Early AI programs, such as the Logic Theorist and General Problem Solver, demonstrated the potential of machines to perform tasks that required human-like reasoning. However, the limitations of early AI systems and the challenges of scaling up these approaches led to a period known as the "AI winter," characterized by reduced funding and interest.

- **Expert Systems and Revival (1980s)**: The development of expert systems in the 1980s marked a revival of AI. Expert systems, such as MYCIN and DENDRAL, used rule-based approaches to emulate the decision-making abilities of human experts in specific domains. These systems found practical applications in medical diagnosis, engineering, and finance.
- **Modern AI and Machine Learning (1990s-Present)**: The resurgence of AI in the 1990s and 2000s was driven by advances in machine learning, a subfield of AI that focuses on developing algorithms that allow machines to learn from data. The availability of large datasets, increased computational power, and the development of new algorithms led to breakthroughs in areas like natural language processing, computer vision, and autonomous systems.

1.2 Types of AI: Narrow AI vs. General AI

Narrow AI (Weak AI)

Narrow AI, also known as Weak AI, refers to AI systems that are designed and trained to perform specific tasks. These systems operate within a limited domain and do not possess general intelligence or understanding. Narrow AI excels at performing well-defined tasks, such as image recognition, language translation, or playing specific games like chess or Go.

Examples of Narrow AI include:

- **Voice Assistants**: AI-powered voice assistants like Siri, Alexa, and Google Assistant can understand and respond to user queries within a predefined scope.
- **Recommendation Systems**: Platforms like Netflix, Amazon, and Spotify use AI algorithms to recommend content based on user preferences and behavior.
- **Autonomous Vehicles**: Self-driving cars use AI to navigate and make decisions based on sensor data and predefined rules.

General AI (Strong AI)

General AI, also known as Strong AI or Artificial General Intelligence (AGI), refers to AI systems that possess the ability to understand, learn, and apply knowledge across a wide range of tasks at a level comparable to human intelligence. General AI systems can reason, plan, solve problems, and exhibit cognitive abilities similar to humans.

While Narrow AI has seen significant advancements and practical applications, General AI remains a theoretical concept. Developing AGI involves overcoming substantial technical and ethical challenges, including creating systems that can understand context, exhibit common sense, and learn continuously from diverse experiences.

1.3 Key Concepts: Machine Learning, Deep Learning, Neural Networks

Machine Learning

Machine learning is a subfield of AI that focuses on developing algorithms that enable machines to learn from data and make predictions or decisions without being explicitly programmed. Machine learning algorithms build models based on sample data, known as training data, to make predictions or decisions without human intervention.

Types of Machine Learning:

- **Supervised Learning**: In supervised learning, the algorithm is trained on labeled data, where each training example is paired with an output label. The goal is to learn a mapping from inputs to outputs. Examples include classification and regression tasks.
- **Unsupervised Learning**: In unsupervised learning, the algorithm is trained on unlabeled data and must find patterns and relationships within the data. Examples include clustering and dimensionality reduction.
- **Reinforcement Learning**: In reinforcement learning, an agent learns to make decisions by taking actions in an environment to maximize cumulative reward. The agent receives feedback in the form of rewards or penalties based on its actions.

Deep Learning
Deep learning is a subset of machine learning that involves neural networks with many layers, known as deep neural networks. Deep learning models are capable of learning hierarchical representations of data, making them particularly effective for tasks such as image and speech recognition.

Key characteristics of deep learning include:

- **Neural Networks**: Deep learning models are based on artificial neural networks, which are inspired by the structure and function of the human brain. These networks consist of layers of interconnected nodes (neurons) that process and transform input data.
- **Automatic Feature Extraction**: Unlike traditional machine learning, where features need to be manually engineered, deep learning models can automatically learn and extract relevant features from raw data.
- **Scalability**: Deep learning models can handle large-scale data and complex tasks, benefiting from increased computational power and large datasets.

Neural Networks
Neural networks are the building blocks of deep learning. They consist of interconnected layers of nodes (neurons) that process input data and produce output predictions. Each connection between neurons has an associated weight, which is adjusted during training to minimize prediction errors.

Types of Neural Networks:

- **Feedforward Neural Networks**: The simplest type of neural network, where data flows in one direction from input to output.
- **Convolutional Neural Networks (CNNs)**: Designed for processing structured grid data, such as images. CNNs use convolutional layers to automatically learn spatial hierarchies of features.
- **Recurrent Neural Networks (RNNs)**: Designed for sequential data, such as time series or natural language. RNNs have connections that form directed cycles, allowing them to maintain memory of previous inputs.

Final Thoughts

Understanding AI is the first step in harnessing its potential to drive business innovation and transformation. By grasping the definitions and history of AI, differentiating between Narrow AI and General AI, and delving into key concepts like machine learning, deep learning, and neural networks, you are better equipped to navigate the complexities of AI and leverage its capabilities effectively.

As you proceed through this book, you will gain deeper insights into implementing AI in various business contexts, from setting objectives and developing models to managing data and ensuring ethical practices. Embrace the journey with curiosity and a commitment to continuous learning, and you will be well-prepared to unlock the transformative power of AI in your organization.

PROMPT - Write a comprehensive and thorough chapter 2 on The Business Case for AI, with subchapters on Benefits of AI: Efficiency, innovation, decision-making; AI in Different Sectors: Finance, healthcare, retail, manufacturing; and Case Studies: Successful AI implementations.

Chapter 2: The Business Case for AI

Artificial Intelligence (AI) is revolutionizing the way businesses operate, offering significant benefits across various sectors. This chapter provides a comprehensive exploration of the business case for AI, focusing on its benefits, applications in different sectors, and real-world case studies of successful AI implementations.

2.1 Benefits of AI: Efficiency, Innovation, Decision-Making

Efficiency

AI can greatly enhance efficiency in various business processes by automating repetitive tasks, optimizing resource allocation, and improving operational workflows. Key benefits include:

- **Automation**: AI-powered automation can handle routine tasks such as data entry, scheduling, and customer service inquiries, freeing up employees to focus on more strategic activities.
- **Process Optimization**: AI algorithms can analyze large datasets to identify inefficiencies and suggest improvements in processes such as supply chain management, inventory control, and production scheduling.
- **Cost Reduction**: By automating tasks and optimizing processes, AI helps reduce operational costs, leading to higher profitability.

Innovation

AI drives innovation by enabling businesses to develop new products and services, enhance customer experiences, and explore new business models. Key benefits include:

- **Product Development**: AI can accelerate product development cycles by analyzing market trends, customer feedback, and design iterations to create innovative products that meet customer needs.
- **Personalization**: AI enables personalized experiences for customers by analyzing their preferences and behavior, leading to tailored recommendations, targeted marketing, and improved customer satisfaction.
- **New Business Models**: AI technologies such as predictive analytics and machine learning can uncover new business opportunities and revenue streams by analyzing market data and identifying emerging trends.

Decision-Making

AI enhances decision-making by providing data-driven insights, predictive analytics, and real-time information. Key benefits include:

- **Data-Driven Insights**: AI can analyze vast amounts of data to uncover patterns, correlations, and trends that inform strategic decision-making.
- **Predictive Analytics**: AI models can forecast future outcomes based on historical data, helping businesses make proactive decisions and mitigate risks.

- **Real-Time Information**: AI systems can provide real-time monitoring and analysis of business operations, enabling managers to make informed decisions quickly and respond to changing conditions.

2.2 AI in Different Sectors: Finance, Healthcare, Retail, Manufacturing

Finance

The finance sector has been at the forefront of AI adoption, leveraging its capabilities to enhance various functions such as risk management, fraud detection, and customer service.

- **Risk Management**: AI algorithms can analyze financial data to assess credit risk, detect anomalies, and predict potential defaults. This helps financial institutions make better lending decisions and manage their portfolios more effectively.
- **Fraud Detection**: AI systems can detect fraudulent activities by analyzing transaction patterns and identifying suspicious behavior in real-time, helping to prevent financial losses.
- **Customer Service**: AI-powered chatbots and virtual assistants can handle customer inquiries, provide personalized financial advice, and streamline the onboarding process for new clients.

Healthcare

AI is transforming healthcare by improving diagnostics, personalized treatment, and operational efficiency.

- **Diagnostics**: AI algorithms can analyze medical images, genetic data, and electronic health records to assist in diagnosing diseases such as cancer, cardiovascular conditions, and neurological disorders. This leads to more accurate and timely diagnoses.
- **Personalized Treatment**: AI can analyze patient data to develop personalized treatment plans, predict treatment outcomes, and identify potential side effects. This enhances patient care and improves treatment efficacy.
- **Operational Efficiency**: AI can optimize hospital operations by predicting patient admissions, managing bed occupancy, and streamlining administrative tasks, leading to improved patient flow and reduced wait times.

Retail

AI is revolutionizing the retail sector by enhancing customer experiences, optimizing supply chains, and driving sales.

- **Customer Experiences**: AI-powered recommendation systems can provide personalized product suggestions based on customer preferences and behavior, leading to increased sales and customer satisfaction.
- **Supply Chain Optimization**: AI can analyze supply chain data to forecast demand, optimize inventory levels, and improve logistics, reducing costs and ensuring timely delivery of products.

- **Sales and Marketing**: AI can enhance marketing strategies by analyzing customer data, segmenting audiences, and predicting buying behavior, enabling targeted and effective marketing campaigns.

Manufacturing

AI is driving innovation and efficiency in the manufacturing sector through predictive maintenance, quality control, and process optimization.

- **Predictive Maintenance**: AI algorithms can predict equipment failures by analyzing sensor data and historical maintenance records, allowing for proactive maintenance and reducing downtime.
- **Quality Control**: AI systems can inspect products in real-time, identifying defects and ensuring consistent quality. This reduces waste and enhances product reliability.
- **Process Optimization**: AI can optimize manufacturing processes by analyzing production data, identifying bottlenecks, and suggesting improvements, leading to increased efficiency and productivity.

2.3 Case Studies: Successful AI Implementations

Finance: JPMorgan Chase

JPMorgan Chase implemented an AI-powered contract analysis platform called COiN (Contract Intelligence). COiN uses machine learning to review legal documents and extract important data points and clauses. This has significantly reduced the time and cost associated with reviewing complex legal contracts, improving efficiency and accuracy in the process.

Healthcare: IBM Watson for Oncology

IBM Watson for Oncology is an AI system designed to assist oncologists in developing personalized treatment plans for cancer patients. The system analyzes patient data, medical literature, and clinical guidelines to provide evidence-based treatment recommendations. This has helped healthcare providers deliver more precise and effective cancer treatments, improving patient outcomes.

Retail: Amazon

Amazon uses AI extensively to enhance its operations and customer experiences. The company's recommendation system leverages machine learning algorithms to analyze customer behavior and preferences, providing personalized product suggestions that drive sales. Additionally, Amazon's AI-powered logistics and supply chain management systems optimize inventory levels, reduce delivery times, and improve operational efficiency.

Manufacturing: Siemens

Siemens implemented an AI-powered predictive maintenance solution for its manufacturing facilities. The system analyzes sensor data from machines to predict potential failures and recommend maintenance actions. This has reduced downtime, improved equipment reliability, and increased overall productivity in Siemens' manufacturing operations.

Final Thoughts

AI offers transformative benefits for businesses across various sectors, enhancing efficiency, driving innovation, and improving decision-making. By understanding the potential applications of AI in finance, healthcare, retail, and manufacturing, and learning from successful case studies, businesses can make informed decisions about integrating AI into their operations.

As you continue through this book, you will gain deeper insights into setting AI objectives, managing data, developing AI models, and ensuring ethical practices. Embrace the opportunities AI presents and approach its implementation with a strategic mindset to unlock its full potential and drive your business forward.

PROMPT -Write a comprehensive, extensive and thorough chapter 3 on Preparing for AI, developing subchapters on Assessing Readiness: Evaluating current capabilities; Setting Goals: Defining objectives for AI implementation; Building a Team: Roles and responsibilities (data scientists, engineers, etc.); and Developing a roadmap: Milestones, timelines and resource allocations.

Chapter 3: Preparing for AI

Implementing AI within an organization is a multifaceted process that requires thorough preparation and strategic planning. This chapter delves into the key components of preparing for AI, including assessing your organization's readiness, setting clear goals, building an effective team, and developing a comprehensive roadmap. Each of these steps is crucial to ensure a smooth and successful AI implementation.

3.1 Assessing Readiness: Evaluating Current Capabilities

Before embarking on an AI journey, it is essential to evaluate your organization's current capabilities and readiness. This a detailed assessment of various factors including technological infrastructure, data availability, and organizational culture.

Here's how to conduct a readiness assessment:

Technological Infrastructure

- **Hardware and Software**: Assess whether your current hardware and software can support AI technologies. This includes evaluating servers, storage solutions, and the capability of existing IT systems to handle large datasets and complex computations.

- **Data Management Systems**: Review the data management systems in place, including databases, data warehouses, and data lakes. Ensure that these systems can store, process, and retrieve data efficiently.
- **Network Capabilities**: Check the network infrastructure to ensure it can handle increased data traffic and connectivity requirements that AI implementations often demand.

Data Availability and Quality

- **Data Inventory**: Conduct an inventory of available data sources. Identify what data is accessible, its format, and its relevance to potential AI projects.
- **Data Quality**: Evaluate the quality of your data. This includes checking for completeness, accuracy, consistency, and timeliness. High-quality data is critical for training reliable AI models.
- **Data Governance**: Ensure that there are robust data governance policies in place to manage data privacy, security, and compliance with regulations.

Organizational Culture and Skills

- **Awareness and Attitude**: Gauge the level of awareness and attitude towards AI within the organization. Are stakeholders and employees open to adopting AI technologies?

- **Skill Levels**: Assess the current skill levels of your workforce in areas such as data science, machine learning, and AI. Identify skill gaps that need to be addressed through training or hiring.
- **Change Management**: Evaluate the organization's capacity to manage change. Successful AI implementation requires adaptability and a willingness to embrace new ways of working.

Financial Readiness

- **Budget Allocation**: Determine the financial resources available for AI projects. Consider the costs of technology, talent acquisition, training, and ongoing maintenance.
- **Investment Horizon**: Understand the investment horizon and return on investment (ROI) expectations. AI projects often require significant upfront investment with returns accruing over time.

3.2 Setting Goals: Defining Objectives for AI Implementation

Clear, well-defined goals are essential for guiding AI initiatives. Setting objectives helps align AI projects with business strategies and ensures that all stakeholders have a common understanding of what the organization aims to achieve.

Aligning with Business Strategy

- **Strategic Priorities**: Identify how AI can support the organization's strategic priorities. For instance, if customer satisfaction is a key focus, AI could be used to enhance customer service through chatbots or personalized recommendations.
- **Value Creation**: Define the value AI is expected to create. This could be in the form of cost savings, revenue growth, improved efficiency, or enhanced customer experiences.

SMART Goals

- **Specific**: Goals should be clear and specific. Instead of a vague goal like "improve customer service," a specific goal could be "reduce customer service response time by 50% using AI chatbots."
- **Measurable**: Establish metrics to measure progress. This could include KPIs such as reduced operational costs, increased sales, or higher customer satisfaction scores.
- **Achievable**: Ensure goals are realistic and achievable given the current resources and constraints. Setting overly ambitious goals can lead to frustration and failure.
- **Relevant**: Goals should be relevant to the overall business strategy and priorities. This ensures that AI initiatives are aligned with the broader organizational objectives.
- **Time-bound**: Set a clear timeline for achieving the goals. This helps in planning and maintaining focus on the end objectives.

Stakeholder Involvement

- **Engage Key Stakeholders**: Involve key stakeholders in the goal-setting process. This includes executives, department heads, and end-users who will be affected by the AI implementation.
- **Communication**: Clearly communicate the goals and objectives to all stakeholders. This ensures everyone understands the purpose and expected outcomes of the AI initiatives.

3.3 Building a Team: Roles and Responsibilities

A successful AI implementation requires a multidisciplinary team with diverse skills and expertise. Building the right team involves identifying the necessary roles, recruiting the right talent, and defining clear responsibilities.

Key Roles in an AI Team
Data Scientists

- **Role**: Data scientists are responsible for developing AI models, analyzing data, and deriving insights. They use statistical techniques, machine learning algorithms, and programming skills to create predictive models.
- **Skills**: Expertise in programming languages (e.g., Python, R), statistical analysis, machine learning frameworks, and data visualization tools.

Data Engineers

- **Role**: Data engineers build and maintain the infrastructure required for data generation, storage, and processing. They ensure that data pipelines are efficient and scalable.
- **Skills**: Proficiency in database management, ETL (Extract, Transform, Load) processes, big data technologies (e.g., Hadoop, Spark), and cloud platforms.

AI/ML Engineers

- **Role**: AI/ML engineers focus on implementing and deploying AI models into production. They work on optimizing algorithms and integrating AI solutions into existing systems.
- **Skills**: Strong programming skills, understanding of machine learning algorithms, experience with AI frameworks (e.g., TensorFlow, PyTorch), and knowledge of software engineering practices.

Domain Experts

- **Role**: Domain experts provide industry-specific knowledge and insights. They help in understanding the context of the data and ensure that AI solutions are relevant and applicable.
- **Skills**: Deep understanding of the specific industry or domain, ability to translate business requirements into technical specifications, and collaboration with technical teams.

Project Managers

- **Role**: Project managers oversee the AI project, ensuring that it stays on track, within budget, and meets the defined objectives. They coordinate between different team members and manage stakeholder expectations.
- **Skills**: Strong organizational and communication skills, experience in project management methodologies (e.g., Agile, Scrum), and ability to manage timelines and resources effectively.

Ethicists and Legal Advisors

- **Role**: Ethicists and legal advisors ensure that AI implementations adhere to ethical standards and legal regulations. They help in navigating compliance issues and addressing ethical concerns.
- **Skills**: Knowledge of AI ethics, familiarity with relevant laws and regulations (e.g., GDPR, CCPA), and ability to provide guidance on ethical AI practices.

Defining Responsibilities

- **Clear Roles**: Clearly define the roles and responsibilities of each team member. This helps in avoiding overlaps and ensures accountability.
- **Collaboration**: Foster a collaborative environment where team members can work together effectively. Encourage open communication and knowledge sharing.

- **Continuous Learning**: Encourage continuous learning and development. AI is a rapidly evolving field, and staying updated with the latest advancements is crucial.

3.4 Developing a Roadmap: Milestones, Timelines, and Resource Allocations

A well-defined roadmap is essential for guiding the AI implementation process. It outlines the key milestones, timelines, and resource allocations, ensuring that the project stays on track and meets its objectives.

Milestones and Timelines
Project Phases

- **Initiation**: Define the project scope, objectives, and key deliverables. This phase includes securing stakeholder buy-in and assembling the project team.
- **Planning**: Develop a detailed project plan, including timelines, milestones, and resource allocations. Identify potential risks and mitigation strategies.
- **Execution**: Implement the project plan, develop AI models, and integrate them into existing systems. Monitor progress and make necessary adjustments.
- **Evaluation**: Evaluate the performance of the AI models, gather feedback, and make improvements. Ensure that the project meets its defined objectives.
- **Deployment**: Deploy the AI models into production, monitor their performance, and ensure ongoing maintenance and support.

Key Milestones

- **Data Collection and Preparation**: Gather and preprocess the data required for training AI models. Ensure data quality and relevance.
- **Model Development**: Develop and train AI models, validate their performance, and make necessary adjustments.
- **System Integration**: Integrate AI models into existing systems, ensuring compatibility and smooth operation.
- **Testing and Evaluation**: Conduct thorough testing to evaluate the performance and reliability of the AI models.
- **Deployment**: Deploy the AI models into production, monitor their performance, and ensure ongoing maintenance.

Resource Allocations
Budget Planning

- **Technology Costs**: Allocate budget for hardware, software, and cloud services required for AI implementation.
- **Talent Acquisition**: Allocate budget for hiring and training the necessary talent, including data scientists, engineers, and domain experts.
- **Operational Costs**: Consider ongoing operational costs, including maintenance, support, and continuous improvements.

Time Management

- **Timeline Development**: Develop a realistic timeline for the AI project, considering the complexity of tasks and potential challenges.
- **Milestone Tracking**: Track progress against the defined milestones, and make necessary adjustments to stay on track.

Risk Management

- **Risk Identification**: Identify potential risks and challenges that may arise during the AI implementation process.
- **Mitigation Strategies**: Develop mitigation strategies to address identified risks and minimize their impact on the project.

Communication and Reporting

- **Stakeholder Communication**: Maintain regular communication with stakeholders, providing updates on progress and addressing any concerns.
- **Progress Reporting**: Develop a reporting mechanism to track and report progress against the defined milestones and objectives.

Final Thoughts

Preparing for AI involves a strategic and methodical approach to ensure successful implementation. By thoroughly assessing readiness, setting clear and achievable goals, building a capable team, and developing a detailed roadmap, organizations can lay a strong foundation for their AI initiatives. This preparation phase is critical as it sets the stage for effective AI deployment, helping to maximize the benefits while minimizing potential risks.

AI holds immense potential to transform businesses, drive innovation, and enhance decision-making processes. However, the journey towards AI adoption requires careful planning, resource allocation, and continuous learning. By investing the time and effort in the preparation phase, organizations can position themselves to harness the full power of AI, leading to sustainable growth and competitive advantage.

As you move forward, remember that the landscape of AI is constantly evolving. Stay informed about the latest advancements, continuously refine your strategies, and be open to adapting your approach based on emerging trends and technologies. With a solid foundation and a commitment to ongoing learning, your organization can successfully navigate the complexities of AI implementation and achieve remarkable outcomes.

PROMPT -Create Chapter 4, on the topic of Data Management, writing subchapters on Importance of Data: The foundation of AI, Data Collection: Methods and best practices, Data Quality: Ensuring accuracy and relevance, Data Governance: Policies and compliance.

Chapter 4: Data Management

Data management is a critical component of any successful AI implementation. The quality, accessibility, and governance of data determine the effectiveness and reliability of AI models. This chapter explores the fundamental aspects of data management, including its importance, methods of data collection, ensuring data quality, and establishing data governance policies.

4.1 Importance of Data: The Foundation of AI

Introduction

Data is the lifeblood of AI. Without high-quality data, AI models cannot learn effectively, leading to inaccurate predictions and poor decision-making. Understanding the importance of data and treating it as a strategic asset is essential for any organization aiming to leverage AI.

Key Points

- **Data as a Strategic Asset**: Data provides the raw material for AI algorithms to learn and make predictions. It enables organizations to gain insights, identify patterns, and make informed decisions.
- **Volume, Variety, and Velocity**: The three Vs of big data (volume, variety, and velocity) describe the characteristics of data that AI models require. Large volumes of data from diverse sources, processed at high speed, enhance the robustness of AI solutions.
- **Impact on Model Performance**: The quality and relevance of data directly impact the performance of AI

models. Clean, accurate, and well-labeled data improve model accuracy, while poor-quality data can lead to biases and errors.

Real-World Examples

- **Retail**: E-commerce platforms use customer transaction data to personalize recommendations, improving customer satisfaction and sales.
- **Healthcare**: Patient data, including medical histories and lab results, enables predictive analytics for better diagnosis and treatment planning.

4.2 Data Collection: Methods and Best Practices

Introduction

Effective data collection methods ensure that AI models have access to the right data at the right time. This subchapter explores various data collection methods and best practices to ensure comprehensive and reliable data gathering.

[

PROMPT - Abound on the data collection methods

Manual Data Entry

Manual data entry involves human operators inputting data into a system. This method is often used when data is not available in a digital format or when the data needs to be collected from physical documents or direct observations.

Applications

- **Surveys and Questionnaires**: Inputting responses collected on paper forms.
- **Laboratory Results**: Entering data from lab tests or medical examinations.
- **Customer Feedback**: Logging customer comments and feedback from physical suggestion boxes.

Advantages

- **Flexibility**: Can be used in various scenarios where automated methods are not feasible.
- **Accuracy**: Human judgment can sometimes ensure better accuracy in interpreting complex or ambiguous data.

Challenges

- **Error-Prone**: Prone to human errors such as typos or misinterpretations.
- **Time-Consuming**: Slow and labor-intensive, making it impractical for large volumes of data.
- **Scalability**: Difficult to scale for large datasets or continuous data collection.

Automated Data Collection

Automated data collection leverages technology to gather data continuously and accurately without human intervention. This method is highly efficient and suitable for environments where data is generated at high volumes and speed.

Applications

- **Internet of Things (IoT)**: Sensors in smart devices collecting data on usage, environment, and performance (e.g., smart meters, wearable health monitors).
- **Web Analytics**: Tracking user interactions on websites through tools like Google Analytics.
- **Transaction Systems**: Capturing data from point-of-sale (POS) systems in retail or financial transactions in banking.

Advantages

- **Efficiency**: Fast and capable of handling large volumes of data.
- **Accuracy**: Reduces human error and increases the reliability of the data.
- **Real-Time**: Enables real-time data collection and processing.

Challenges

- **Initial Setup**: Requires investment in technology and infrastructure.

- **Maintenance**: Ongoing maintenance and updates are necessary to ensure continued accuracy and functionality.
- **Data Privacy**: Ensuring compliance with data protection regulations and securing collected data.

Web Scraping

Web scraping involves using automated scripts or tools to extract data from websites. This method is useful for gathering publicly available information from the internet.

Applications

- **Market Research**: Collecting competitor pricing, product information, and customer reviews.
- **News Aggregation**: Extracting news articles and updates from various sources.
- **Academic Research**: Gathering information from scientific publications and online databases.

Advantages

- **Access to Public Data**: Easily collects large amounts of data from public sources.
- **Automated**: Once set up, it can continuously gather data without manual intervention.
- **Cost-Effective**: Low operational costs compared to manual data collection.

Challenges

- **Legal Issues**: Must comply with website terms of service and data protection laws.
- **Data Quality**: Websites may change their structure, breaking the scraping scripts.
- **Ethical Considerations**: Ensuring that data collection does not violate privacy or ethical guidelines.

APIs (Application Programming Interfaces)

APIs enable different software systems to communicate and share data. They provide a structured way to access data from external sources, ensuring data consistency and integration.

Applications

- **Social Media**: Accessing data from platforms like Twitter, Facebook, and LinkedIn.
- **Financial Services**: Integrating with banking systems for transaction data.
- **Weather Services**: Collecting weather data for predictive analytics.

Advantages

- **Consistency**: Provides structured and consistent data formats.
- **Reliability**: APIs are maintained by providers, ensuring data accuracy and uptime.
- **Integration**: Simplifies the integration of multiple data sources into a single system.

Challenges

- **Dependency**: Relying on third-party providers for data availability and quality.
- **Rate Limits**: APIs often have usage limits, which can restrict data collection volume.
- **Complexity**: Requires technical expertise to implement and manage API integrations.

Surveys and Questionnaires

Surveys and questionnaires are tools for collecting data directly from individuals. They can be administered in various formats, including paper, online, or through interviews.

Applications

- **Customer Satisfaction**: Collecting feedback on products, services, or experiences.
- **Market Research**: Understanding consumer preferences, behaviors, and demographics.
- **Employee Engagement**: Gauging employee satisfaction and organizational climate.

Advantages

- **Direct Feedback**: Provides direct insights from the target audience.
- **Customizable**: Can be tailored to specific research questions and objectives.
- **Qualitative Data**: Gathers detailed qualitative data that is not easily captured through automated methods.

Challenges

- **Response Rates**: Achieving high response rates can be challenging.
- **Bias**: Responses may be biased due to the way questions are phrased or the context in which they are asked.
- **Data Quality**: Ensuring the accuracy and honesty of responses can be difficult.

Best Practices for Data Collection

1. **Define Clear Objectives**: Understand the specific data requirements based on AI objectives. Define what data is needed and why.
2. **Ensure Data Privacy and Security**: Protect data during collection, storage, and transmission. Comply with data protection regulations and obtain necessary consents.
3. **Use Multiple Sources**: Combine data from various sources to increase data richness and reliability. This helps in building a comprehensive dataset.
4. **Validate and Clean Data**: Implement validation checks at the point of data entry. Regularly clean data to remove errors, duplicates, and inconsistencies.
5. **Document Data Collection Processes**: Maintain detailed documentation of data collection methods, sources, and processing steps to ensure transparency and reproducibility.

By understanding and effectively implementing these data collection methods, organizations can ensure that their AI models are built on a robust and reliable foundation. High-quality data collection is essential for deriving accurate insights and achieving the desired outcomes from AI initiatives.

] [

PROMPT - Abound on data quality

4.3 Data Quality: Ensuring Accuracy and Relevance

Introduction
Data quality is the cornerstone of effective AI implementation. The accuracy, completeness, consistency, timeliness, and relevance of data directly impact the performance and reliability of AI models. Ensuring high data quality involves a series of processes and practices aimed at maintaining and enhancing the integrity of the data used for AI.

Key Aspects of Data Quality
Accuracy
Data accuracy refers to how closely the data values match the true values or real-world scenarios they represent.
Accurate data ensures that AI models make precise predictions and decisions.

- **Best Practices**:
    - **Data Entry Validation**: Implement validation rules to check data accuracy during entry.

- **Regular Audits**: Conduct periodic data audits to identify and correct inaccuracies.
- **Cross-Verification**: Compare data against reliable external sources to ensure correctness.

Completeness

Data completeness indicates whether all necessary data points are present and accounted for.

Incomplete data can lead to biased models and unreliable outcomes.

- **Best Practices**:
    - **Mandatory Fields**: Mark essential fields as mandatory in data collection forms.
    - **Imputation Techniques**: Use statistical methods to fill in missing values where appropriate.
    - **Data Source Integration**: Aggregate data from multiple sources to fill gaps.

Consistency

Data consistency refers to the uniformity of data across different sources and systems. Consistent data ensures that AI models are trained on uniform and reliable datasets.

- **Best Practices**:
    - **Standardization**: Apply consistent data formats, units, and naming conventions.
    - **Data Harmonization**: Resolve discrepancies between different data sources.

- **Automated Consistency Checks**: Use tools to automatically identify and rectify inconsistencies.

Timeliness

Data timeliness measures how up-to-date the data is. Timely data is crucial for AI models that rely on current information for real-time decision-making.

- **Best Practice**s:
    - **Real-Time Data Feeds**: Implement real-time data collection and processing systems.
    - **Regular Updates**: Schedule regular data updates to ensure recency.
    - **Archival Policies**: Define clear policies for archiving outdated data and replacing it with fresh data.

Relevance

Data relevance assesses whether the data collected is pertinent to the problem at hand. Relevant data ensures that AI models focus on the right variables and make meaningful predictions.

- **Best Practices**:
    - **Clear Objectives**: Align data collection with specific AI objectives.
    - **Domain Expertise**: Involve domain experts to ensure the relevance of the data.
    - **Continuous Review**: Regularly review and update data collection criteria to maintain relevance.

Methods to Ensure Data Quality
Data Validation
Data validation involves checking data for accuracy and completeness at the point of entry.

- **Techniques**:
    - **Format Checks**: Ensure data conforms to specified formats (e.g., dates, numbers).
    - **Range Checks**: Verify that data values fall within expected ranges.
    - **Consistency Checks**: Cross-verify data between related fields (e.g., start and end dates).

Data Cleaning
Data cleaning, or data cleansing, involves removing errors, duplicates, and inconsistencies from datasets.

- **Techniques**:
    - **Duplicate Removal**: Identify and remove duplicate records.
    - **Error Correction**: Correct obvious errors and anomalies in data.
    - **Normalization**: Standardize data formats and units.

Data Enrichment
Data enrichment involves enhancing existing data by adding relevant information from external sources.

- **Techniques**:
    - **Third-Party Data**: Integrate data from reputable external sources to add context.
    - **Derived Variables**: Create new variables from existing data to add value (e.g., calculating customer lifetime value from transaction data).

Quality Monitoring

Continuous monitoring of data quality helps maintain high standards and quickly address any issues that arise.

- **Techniques**:
    - **Automated Quality Checks**: Use automated tools to regularly check data for quality issues.
    - **Dashboards and Alerts**: Implement dashboards to visualize data quality metrics and set up alerts for anomalies.
    - **User Feedback**: Collect feedback from data users to identify and rectify quality issues.

User Feedback and Collaboration

Engaging with data users and domain experts helps identify and address data quality issues from a practical perspective.

- **Techniques**:
    - **Workshops and Training**: Conduct workshops to educate users on data quality standards and practices.

- o **Feedback Loops**: Establish mechanisms for users to report data quality issues and suggest improvements.
- o **Collaborative Platforms**: Use collaborative tools to facilitate communication and knowledge sharing among data stakeholders.

Ensuring Data Quality in Practice
Real-World Applications

- **Healthcare**: Ensuring the quality of patient data, including medical histories and test results, to improve diagnostic accuracy and treatment outcomes.
- **Finance**: Maintaining high-quality transaction data to prevent fraud, ensure compliance, and support financial analytics.
- **Retail**: Keeping customer data accurate and up-to-date to enhance personalized marketing and improve customer experience.

Case Study:
Improving Data Quality in a Retail Environment

- **Problem**: A retail company faced challenges with inconsistent and incomplete customer data, leading to ineffective marketing campaigns and poor customer insights.
- **Solution**:
  - o **Data Standardization**: Implemented standard data formats and naming conventions across all customer touchpoints.

- o **Automated Data Cleaning**: Deployed automated tools to regularly clean and deduplicate customer records.
- o **Data Enrichment**: Integrated third-party demographic data to enhance customer profiles.
- o **Quality Monitoring**: Set up dashboards to monitor data quality metrics and alert the data management team to any issues.
- **Outcome**: Improved data quality led to more effective marketing campaigns, increased customer engagement, and better business insights.

Maintaining high data quality is a continuous and evolving process. By implementing robust data validation, cleaning, enrichment, and monitoring practices, organizations can ensure that their AI models are trained on reliable, accurate, and relevant data, leading to more effective and trustworthy AI solutions.

]

4.4 Data Governance: Policies and Compliance

Introduction
Data governance involves the policies, procedures, and standards that ensure the effective and ethical management of data within an organization. This subchapter discusses the importance of data governance, key policies, and compliance requirements.

Importance of Data Governance

- **Ensures Data Integrity and Security**: Protects data from unauthorized access and ensures its integrity through standardized procedures.
- **Regulatory Compliance**: Helps organizations comply with data protection regulations such as GDPR, CCPA, and HIPAA, avoiding legal penalties.
- **Promotes Data Consistency**: Establishes consistent data definitions, formats, and standards across the organization, facilitating better data integration and analysis.
- **Enhances Data Usability**: Ensures that data is accessible, accurate, and relevant, improving its usability for AI applications and decision-making.

Key Data Governance Policies

- **Data Access and Security**: Define who can access data and under what conditions. Implement role-based access controls and encryption to protect sensitive data.
- **Data Quality Management**: Establish policies for data validation, cleaning, and monitoring to maintain high data quality.
- **Data Lifecycle Management**: Define procedures for data collection, storage, usage, archiving, and disposal. Ensure data is retained only as long as necessary.
- **Data Privacy and Compliance**: Implement policies to ensure compliance with data protection regulations. Conduct regular audits and assessments to identify and mitigate risks.

- **Data Stewardship**: Assign data stewards responsible for managing data quality and governance within specific domains or departments.

Compliance Requirements

- **General Data Protection Regulation (GDPR)**: Requires organizations to protect the personal data and privacy of EU citizens. Key requirements include data subject rights, breach notifications, and data protection impact assessments (DPIAs).
- **California Consumer Privacy Act (CCPA)**: Grants California residents the right to know about and control their personal data. Organizations must provide transparency, enable data access requests, and ensure data deletion upon request.
- **Health Insurance Portability and Accountability Act (HIPAA)**: Protects sensitive patient health information in the US. Organizations must implement safeguards to ensure the confidentiality, integrity, and security of healthcare data.

Best Practices for Data Governance

- **Establish a Data Governance Framework**: Develop a comprehensive framework that outlines roles, responsibilities, policies, and procedures for data management.
- **Engage Stakeholders**: Involve key stakeholders from various departments to ensure buy-in and collaboration on data governance initiatives.

- **Continuous Improvement**: Regularly review and update data governance policies and procedures to adapt to changing regulations and organizational needs.
- **Training and Awareness**: Conduct training programs to educate employees about data governance policies, data protection practices, and their responsibilities.
- **Leverage Technology**: Use data governance tools and platforms to automate compliance checks, monitor data quality, and manage data access and security.

By implementing robust data management practices, organizations can ensure that their AI initiatives are built on a solid foundation of high-quality, well-governed data. This chapter provides a comprehensive guide to understanding the importance of data, best practices for data collection, methods to maintain data quality, and the essentials of data governance.

PROMPT - Create and abound on a chapter 5 on Choosing the Right AI Solutions, with subchapters on Types of AI Technologies: Natural language processing, computer vision, predictive analytics; Build vs. Buy: Pros and cons of in-house development vs. third-party solutions; and Evaluating Vendors: Criteria for selecting AI providers.

Chapter 5: Choosing the Right AI Solutions

Selecting the appropriate AI solutions for your organization is a crucial step that can significantly impact the success of your AI initiatives. This chapter explores the various types of AI technologies, the decision-making process between building in-house solutions versus buying third-party offerings, and the essential criteria for evaluating AI vendors.

5.1 Types of AI Technologies: Natural Language Processing, Computer Vision, Predictive Analytics

Introduction

Different AI technologies cater to various business needs and applications. Understanding these technologies and their use cases helps organizations choose the most suitable solutions for their specific requirements.

Natural Language Processing (NLP)

- **Overview**: NLP focuses on the interaction between computers and human language. It enables machines to understand, interpret, and respond to human language in a meaningful way.
- **Applications**:
    - **Chatbots and Virtual Assistants**: Automating customer service and support.
    - **Sentiment Analysis**: Gauging public opinion and customer sentiments from social media and reviews.

- **Language Translation**: Translating text from one language to another.
- **Document Processing**: Extracting information from unstructured text data.

- **Advantages**:
    - **Enhanced Customer Interaction**: Improves customer engagement through automated, natural conversations.
    - **Insight Extraction**: Helps in extracting valuable insights from vast amounts of text data.
    - **Efficiency**: Automates repetitive tasks like customer inquiries and document processing.
- **Challenges**:
    - **Context Understanding**: Difficulty in understanding context and nuances of human language.
    - **Language Diversity**: Handling multiple languages and dialects.
    - **Data Privacy**: Ensuring the privacy of user data in language processing applications.

Computer Vision

- **Overview**: Computer vision enables machines to interpret and make decisions based on visual inputs from the world, such as images and videos.
- **Applications**:
    - **Image Recognition**: Identifying objects, people, and scenes in images.
    - **Facial Recognition**: Verifying identities for security and authentication purposes.

- - **Quality Inspection**: Automated inspection and defect detection in manufacturing.
  - **Autonomous Vehicles**: Enabling self-driving cars to perceive and navigate their environment.
- **Advantages**:
  - **Automation**: Reduces the need for manual visual inspection and monitoring.
  - **Accuracy**: Enhances the precision of tasks like defect detection and identification.
  - **Scalability**: Can process and analyze vast amounts of visual data quickly.
- **Challenges**:
  - **Data Requirements**: Requires large datasets for training models.
  - **Privacy Concerns**: Issues related to surveillance and data privacy.
  - **Computational Power**: High computational resources needed for processing and analysis.

Predictive Analytics

- **Overview**: Predictive analytics uses statistical algorithms and machine learning techniques to identify the likelihood of future outcomes based on historical data.
- **Applications**:
  - **Demand Forecasting**: Predicting future product demand to optimize inventory and supply chain.
  - **Customer Churn**: Identifying customers at risk of leaving and implementing retention strategies.

- o **Risk Management**: Assessing risks in finance, insurance, and healthcare.
- o **Personalized Marketing**: Recommending products or services based on customer behavior and preferences.
- **Advantages**:
    - o **Proactive Decision-Making**: Enables organizations to anticipate and respond to future trends and events.
    - o **Efficiency**: Optimizes operations and resources by predicting demand and risk.
    - o **Customer Insights**: Enhances understanding of customer behavior and preferences.
- **Challenges**:
    - o **Data Quality**: Relies heavily on the quality and accuracy of historical data.
    - o **Model Complexity**: Requires sophisticated models and algorithms, which can be complex to develop and maintain.
    - o **Integration**: Challenges in integrating predictive analytics with existing systems and processes.

5.2 Build vs. Buy: Pros and Cons of In-House Development vs. Third-Party Solutions

Introduction
Organizations face a crucial decision when implementing AI solutions: whether to build them in-house or purchase them from third-party vendors. Each approach has its advantages and challenges, and the choice depends on various factors such as budget, expertise, and specific needs.

In-House Development
- **Pros**:
    - **Customization**: Solutions can be tailored to meet specific business requirements and workflows.
    - **Control**: Full control over the development process, data security, and intellectual property.
    - **Integration**: Easier to integrate with existing systems and processes.
    - **Flexibility**: Ability to make changes and improvements as needed without relying on external vendors.
- **Cons**:
    - **Cost**: High initial investment in terms of time, money, and resources.
    - **Expertise**: Requires a skilled team of AI specialists, data scientists, and engineers.
    - **Time-Consuming**: Longer development cycles compared to off-the-shelf solutions.

- Maintenance: Ongoing maintenance and updates are the organization's responsibility.

Third-Party Solutions
- **Pros**:
    - **Speed**: Faster implementation as the solutions are ready-made.
    - **Cost-Effective**: Lower upfront costs compared to building in-house, especially for smaller organizations.
    - **Expertise**: Access to the vendor's expertise and support, reducing the need for in-house specialists.
    - **Scalability**: Vendors often provide scalable solutions that can grow with the organization.
- **Cons**:
    - **Customization Limitations**: Off-the-shelf solutions may not fully meet specific business needs.
    - **Dependency**: Reliance on external vendors for updates, support, and maintenance.
    - **Integration Challenges**: Potential difficulties in integrating with existing systems and data sources.
    - **Data Privacy**: Concerns about data security and privacy when sharing data with third-party providers.

Decision Factors

- **Business Needs**: Assess whether your requirements are unique and complex enough to justify a custom solution.
- **Budget**: Consider the total cost of ownership, including development, maintenance, and vendor fees.
- **Timeline**: Evaluate the urgency of the solution and how quickly it needs to be deployed.
- **Expertise**: Determine whether your organization has the necessary expertise or if it can be acquired.
- **Scalability**: Consider future growth and whether the solution can scale accordingly.

5.3 Evaluating Vendors: Criteria for Selecting AI Providers

Choosing the right AI vendor is critical to the success of your AI projects. A thorough evaluation process helps ensure that the vendor's solutions align with your business objectives and technical requirements. This subchapter outlines key criteria for selecting AI providers.

Vendor Evaluation Criteria
Technical Expertise

- **AI Capabilities**: Assess the vendor's AI technologies and their relevance to your needs (e.g., NLP, computer vision, predictive analytics).

- **Innovation**: Look for vendors that demonstrate continuous innovation and improvements in their AI offerings.
- **Performance**: Evaluate the performance and accuracy of the vendor's AI models through demos, case studies, and pilot projects.

Reputation and Experience

- **Track Record**: Check the vendor's track record and experience in your industry. Look for case studies, testimonials, and references.
- **Customer Reviews**: Read reviews and feedback from other customers to gauge satisfaction and reliability.
- **Partnerships**: Consider the vendor's partnerships with other technology providers and industry leaders.

Customization and Flexibility

- **Customization Options**: Determine the level of customization available to tailor the solution to your specific needs.
- **Scalability**: Ensure that the solution can scale with your business growth and evolving requirements.
- **Integration**: Assess the ease of integrating the solution with your existing systems and workflows.

Data Security and Privacy

- **Compliance**: Verify that the vendor complies with relevant data protection regulations (e.g., GDPR, CCPA).
- **Security Measures**: Evaluate the vendor's data security measures, including encryption, access controls, and incident response plans.
- **Data Ownership**: Clarify data ownership and usage rights to ensure your organization's data remains secure and confidential.

Support and Maintenance

- **Customer Support**: Assess the quality and availability of the vendor's customer support, including response times and support channels.
- **Training and Onboarding**: Consider the vendor's training and onboarding programs to ensure smooth adoption and usage of the solution.
- **Maintenance and Updates**: Evaluate the vendor's maintenance and update policies to ensure the solution remains up-to-date and functional.

Cost and Pricing

- **Pricing Model**: Understand the vendor's pricing model, including subscription fees, usage-based charges, and any additional costs.

- **Total Cost of Ownership**: Consider the total cost of ownership, including initial setup, customization, support, and ongoing maintenance.
- **ROI**: Assess the potential return on investment (ROI) by comparing the costs against the expected benefits and savings.

Vendor Due Diligence Process

1. **Research**: Conduct thorough research on potential vendors, including their websites, whitepapers, and industry reports.
2. **RFP/RFI**: Issue a Request for Proposal (RFP) or Request for Information (RFI) to gather detailed information from vendors.
3. **Demos and Trials**: Request demos and pilot projects to evaluate the vendor's solution in a real-world context.
4. **References**: Contact references provided by the vendor to gather insights into their experiences and satisfaction.
5. **Contract Negotiation**: Carefully review and negotiate the contract terms, including service level agreements (SLAs), data ownership, and exit clauses.

Conclusion

Choosing the right AI solutions involves understanding the types of AI technologies available, making informed decisions between building in-house and purchasing third-party solutions, and carefully evaluating vendors.

PROMPT - Thoroughly develop a chapter 6 on Developing AI Models, with subchapters on Machine Learning Basics: Supervised, unsupervised, and reinforcement learning; Model Training: Data preparation, training, validation, and testing; and Tools and Frameworks: TensorFlow, PyTorch, Scikit-Learn, etc.

Chapter 6: Developing AI Models

Creating robust AI models is a critical step in leveraging artificial intelligence for business applications. This chapter delves into the essentials of machine learning, the process of training AI models, and the tools and frameworks that facilitate model development.

6.1 Machine Learning Basics: Supervised, Unsupervised, and Reinforcement Learning

Introduction

Machine learning (ML) is a subset of AI that focuses on building systems that can learn from and make decisions based on data. Understanding the different types of machine learning is fundamental to developing effective AI models.

Supervised Learning

- **Definition**: Supervised learning involves training a model on a labeled dataset, where the input data is paired with the correct output. The model learns to map inputs to outputs by finding patterns in the data.
- **Applications**:
    - **Classification**: Assigning labels to inputs (e.g., spam detection in emails).
    - **Regression**: Predicting continuous values (e.g., house price prediction).

- **Advantages**:
  - **Accuracy**: Often more accurate due to the availability of labeled data.
  - **Interpretability**: Models can be easily understood and interpreted.
- **Challenges**:
  - **Data Requirements**: Requires large amounts of labeled data, which can be expensive and time-consuming to obtain.
  - **Overfitting**: Models can become too specialized to the training data and perform poorly on new data.

Unsupervised Learning

- **Definition**: Unsupervised learning involves training a model on data without labeled responses. The model tries to find hidden patterns or intrinsic structures in the input data.
- **Applications**:
  - **Clustering**: Grouping similar data points together (e.g., customer segmentation).
  - **Dimensionality Reduction**: Reducing the number of features in the data (e.g., principal component analysis).
- **Advantages**:
  - **Data Efficiency**: Can work with unlabeled data, which is easier to obtain.
  - **Discovery of Hidden Patterns**: Can reveal unknown patterns and structures in the data.
  -

- **Challenges**:
    - **Interpretability**: Results can be harder to interpret compared to supervised learning.
    - **Evaluation**: Lack of clear metrics to evaluate model performance.

Reinforcement Learning

- **Definition**: Reinforcement learning (RL) involves training a model to make a sequence of decisions by rewarding or punishing the model based on its actions. The model learns to maximize cumulative rewards over time.
- **Applications**:
    - **Game Playing**: Training agents to play games like Go and chess.
    - **Robotics**: Teaching robots to perform tasks through trial and error.
- **Advantages**:
    - **Dynamic Learning**: Can adapt to changing environments and learn complex behaviors.
    - **Long-Term Optimization**: Focuses on long-term rewards rather than immediate gains.
- **Challenges**:
    - **Complexity**: Requires careful design of reward systems and can be computationally intensive.
    - **Exploration vs. Exploitation**: Balancing the need to explore new strategies versus exploiting known ones.

6.2 Model Training: Data Preparation, Training, Validation, and Testing

Introduction
Model training is the process of teaching an AI model to make accurate predictions or decisions based on data. This involves several stages, including data preparation, training, validation, and testing.

Data Preparation
- **Data Collection**: Gathering relevant and high-quality data from various sources.
    - **Structured Data**: Data organized in a defined manner, such as databases and spreadsheets.
    - **Unstructured Data**: Data without a predefined format, such as text, images, and videos.
- **Data Cleaning**: Removing or correcting errors, inconsistencies, and duplicates in the data.
    - **Handling Missing Values**: Techniques like imputation or removing rows/columns with missing data.
    - **Outlier Detection**: Identifying and handling outliers that can skew the model.
- **Data Transformation**: Converting data into a suitable format for analysis.
    - **Normalization**: Scaling features to a standard range.
    - **Encoding**: Converting categorical data into numerical format (e.g., one-hot encoding).

- **Data Splitting**: Dividing the dataset into training, validation, and test sets.
    - **Training Set**: Used to train the model.
    - **Validation Set**: Used to tune model parameters and prevent overfitting.
    - **Test Set**: Used to evaluate the final model performance.

Training
- **Algorithm Selection**: Choosing the appropriate machine learning algorithm based on the problem type (e.g., classification, regression).
    - **Linear Models**: Linear regression, logistic regression.
    - **Tree-Based Models**: Decision trees, random forests.
    - **Neural Networks**: Deep learning models for complex tasks.
- **Hyperparameter Tuning**: Adjusting algorithm parameters to optimize model performance.
    - **Grid Search**: Testing a range of parameter combinations.
    - **Random Search**: Randomly sampling parameter values.
- **Model Training**: Feeding the training data to the algorithm and adjusting parameters to minimize the error.
    - **Loss Function**: A function that measures the error between predicted and actual values.
    - **Optimization Algorithm**: Techniques like gradient descent to minimize the loss function.

Validation

- **Cross-Validation**: A technique to evaluate model performance by dividing the data into multiple folds and training/testing the model on different subsets.
    - **K-Fold Cross-Validation**: Dividing the data into K subsets and performing training/testing K times, each time using a different subset as the validation set.
- **Performance Metrics**: Evaluating model performance using various metrics.
    - **Accuracy**: Percentage of correct predictions (for classification).
    - **Precision and Recall**: Metrics for evaluating model performance on imbalanced datasets.
    - **Mean Squared Error (MSE)**: Commonly used for regression tasks.

Testing

- **Final Evaluation**: Assessing model performance on the test set to ensure it generalizes well to new data.
- **Overfitting and Underfitting**: Balancing model complexity to avoid overfitting (too complex) and underfitting (too simple).
    - **Overfitting**: When the model performs well on training data but poorly on new data.
    - **Underfitting**: When the model performs poorly on both training and new data.
- **Model Deployment**: Preparing the model for production use, including integration with existing systems and ensuring scalability.

6.3 Tools and Frameworks: TensorFlow, PyTorch, Scikit-Learn, etc.

Introduction
Several tools and frameworks are available to streamline the development, training, and deployment of AI models. These tools provide powerful capabilities and libraries that simplify the complexities of AI model development.

TensorFlow

- **Overview**: TensorFlow is an open-source machine learning framework developed by Google. It provides a comprehensive ecosystem for building and deploying machine learning models.
- **Key Features**:
    - **Eager Execution**: Allows for immediate evaluation of operations, making debugging and development easier.
    - **TensorFlow Hub**: A repository of reusable machine learning modules.
    - **TensorFlow Extended (TFX)**: A suite of tools for deploying production-ready ML pipelines.
- **Use Cases**:
    - **Image Classification**: Training models for object detection and image recognition.
    - **Natural Language Processing**: Building NLP models for text classification and sentiment analysis.

- **Time Series Analysis**: Developing models for forecasting and anomaly detection.

PyTorch

- **Overview**: PyTorch is an open-source deep learning framework developed by Facebook's AI Research lab. It is known for its flexibility and ease of use, particularly in research and prototyping.
- **Key Features**:
  - **Dynamic Computation Graphs**: Allows for more flexibility in model building and debugging.
  - **TorchScript**: Enables the transition from research to production by providing an intermediate representation of models.
  - **Rich Ecosystem**: Includes libraries such as torchvision for computer vision and torchtext for NLP.
- **Use Cases**:
  - **Research**: Widely used in academic research due to its flexibility and ease of use.
  - **Computer Vision**: Developing models for tasks like image segmentation and object detection.
  - **Reinforcement Learning**: Implementing RL algorithms and training agents.

Scikit-Learn

- **Overview**: Scikit-Learn is a Python library for machine learning that provides simple and efficient tools for data mining and data analysis.
- **Key Features**:
    o **Simple API**: Easy-to-use interface for performing standard ML tasks.
    o **Wide Range of Algorithms**: Implements a variety of machine learning algorithms, including classification, regression, clustering, and dimensionality reduction.
    o **Integration**: Seamlessly integrates with other scientific Python libraries like NumPy and pandas.
- **Use Cases**:
    o **Data Preprocessing**: Providing tools for data transformation and feature extraction.
    o **Model Training**: Implementing machine learning algorithms for various tasks.
    o **Model Evaluation**: Offering metrics and tools for model evaluation and validation.

Other Notable Tools and Frameworks

- **Keras**: A high-level neural networks API, written in Python and capable of running on top of TensorFlow, CNTK, or Theano. Known for its user-friendliness and modularity.
- **Hugging Face Transformers**: A library for state-of-the-art natural language processing, providing

- pre-trained models for tasks like text classification, translation, and summarization.
- **OpenCV**: An open-source computer vision and machine learning software library for real-time applications.
- **Apache Spark MLlib**: A scalable machine learning library that provides various algorithms for classification, regression, clustering, and collaborative filtering. It is designed to work seamlessly with big data and distributed computing environments.
- **XGBoost**: An optimized gradient boosting library designed for speed and performance, widely used for structured/tabular data.
- **LightGBM**: A fast, distributed, high-performance gradient boosting framework based on decision tree algorithms, suitable for large-scale data processing.
- **CatBoost**: A gradient boosting library that handles categorical features automatically, often used for classification and regression tasks.

Conclusion

Selecting the right tools and frameworks is essential for developing effective AI models. These tools provide the necessary capabilities to preprocess data, train models, and deploy them efficiently. The choice of tool depends on the specific requirements of the project, including the type of data, the complexity of the model, and the production environment.

6.4 Key Considerations in AI Model Development

Introduction
Developing effective AI models involves more than just selecting algorithms and frameworks. It requires careful planning and consideration of various factors that can impact the model's performance and deployment.

Data Privacy and Security

- **Importance**: Ensuring that data privacy and security are maintained throughout the AI development process is critical. This includes adhering to regulations such as GDPR and CCPA.
- **Best Practices**:
    - **Data Anonymization**: Removing or encrypting personally identifiable information (PII).
    - **Access Control**: Implementing strict access controls to limit who can view and manipulate the data.
    - **Secure Storage**: Using secure methods to store data, such as encryption and secure cloud storage solutions.

Ethical Considerations
- **Bias and Fairness**: AI models can inadvertently learn and perpetuate biases present in the training data. It's crucial to identify and mitigate these biases to ensure fairness.

- - Techniques:
    - - **Bias Detection**: Regularly evaluate the model for biases and take corrective measures.
    - - **Fairness Metrics**: Implement fairness metrics to monitor and ensure equitable outcomes.
- - **Transparency and Explainability**: Stakeholders need to understand how AI models make decisions, especially in high-stakes scenarios such as healthcare and finance.
  - - Techniques:
    - - **Model Explainability Tools**: Use tools like LIME and SHAP to interpret model predictions.
    - - **Transparent Algorithms**: Prefer algorithms that are inherently interpretable.

Scalability and Performance

- - **Importance**: AI models should be scalable and perform efficiently in production environments.
- - **Best Practices**:
  - - **Optimization**: Optimize model performance for speed and resource utilization.
  - - **Distributed Computing**: Use distributed computing frameworks like Apache Spark for large-scale data processing.

- **Cloud Services**: Leverage cloud services for scalable infrastructure, such as AWS SageMaker, Google AI Platform, and Azure Machine Learning.

Model Maintenance and Monitoring

- **Importance**: Continuous monitoring and maintenance of AI models are essential to ensure they remain accurate and relevant over time.
- **Best Practices**:
  - **Model Drift Detection**: Monitor for changes in data distribution that can affect model performance.
  - **Regular Retraining**: Retrain models periodically with new data to maintain accuracy.
  - **Performance Metrics**: Continuously track key performance metrics to detect and address issues promptly.

Conclusion

Developing AI models is a comprehensive process that involves understanding machine learning fundamentals, effectively training models, and utilizing the right tools and frameworks. Additionally, key considerations such as data privacy, ethical implications, scalability, and ongoing maintenance are critical to the success and sustainability of AI initiatives. By adhering to these principles and best practices, businesses can create robust and impactful AI solutions that drive innovation and deliver significant value.

PROMPT - Go deep on a chapter 7: Integration and Deployment, developing subchapters on System Integration: Embedding AI into existing systems; Deployment Strategies: On-premise vs. cloud, hybrid solutions; and Monitoring and Maintenance: Ensuring ongoing performance and improvements.

Chapter 7: Integration and Deployment

Integrating and deploying AI models is a critical phase in realizing the business value of AI solutions. This chapter explores how to embed AI into existing systems, different deployment strategies, and the importance of monitoring and maintaining AI systems to ensure ongoing performance and improvements.

7.1 System Integration: Embedding AI into Existing Systems

Introduction

Integrating AI models into existing systems can be challenging but is essential for leveraging AI's full potential. This involves embedding AI capabilities into current workflows, ensuring compatibility, and minimizing disruptions.

Understanding Existing Systems

- **System Architecture**: Analyze the current system architecture to identify where AI can be integrated. This includes understanding data flow, key components, and existing technologies.
- **Integration Points**: Determine the points of integration where AI can add the most value, such as enhancing decision-making processes, automating tasks, or providing advanced analytics.

Integration Methods
- **APIs and Microservices**: Use APIs (Application Programming Interfaces) and microservices to integrate AI models with existing systems.
    - **APIs**: Allow different systems to communicate with each other. AI models can be exposed as APIs, enabling other applications to call these models for predictions or insights.
    - **Microservices**: Decompose applications into smaller, independent services. AI functionalities can be implemented as microservices, making them easier to integrate and scale.
- **Middleware**: Implement middleware solutions to facilitate communication and data exchange between AI models and existing systems.
    - **Message Queues**: Use message queues like RabbitMQ or Apache Kafka to handle asynchronous communication between components.
    - **ETL Pipelines**: Create ETL (Extract, Transform, Load) pipelines to preprocess data before feeding it into AI models.

Data Integration

- **Data Sources**: Identify and connect to various data sources required for AI models, such as databases, data warehouses, and external APIs.
- **Data Transformation**: Ensure data is transformed into the appropriate format and structure needed by AI models.

- **Real-time vs. Batch Processing**: Decide whether AI models will process data in real-time or through batch processing, depending on the use case requirements.

Security and Compliance

- **Data Privacy**: Ensure data privacy and security during integration. Implement encryption, anonymization, and secure access controls.
- **Regulatory Compliance**: Adhere to relevant regulations and standards, such as GDPR, HIPAA, or industry-specific guidelines.

Testing and Validation

- **Integration Testing**: Conduct thorough integration testing to ensure AI models work seamlessly with existing systems. Test for functionality, performance, and security.
- **User Acceptance Testing (UAT)**: Involve end-users in testing to validate that the integrated AI solution meets their needs and expectations.

7.2 Deployment Strategies: On-Premise vs. Cloud, Hybrid Solutions

Introduction
Choosing the right deployment strategy is crucial for the successful implementation of AI solutions. This section explores the pros and cons of different deployment approaches, including on-premise, cloud, and hybrid solutions.

On-Premise Deployment

- **Overview**: On-premise deployment involves hosting AI solutions within the organization's own infrastructure.
- **Advantages**:
    - **Data Control**: Full control over data and infrastructure, which can be crucial for sensitive data.
    - **Customization**: Greater flexibility to customize and optimize the environment for specific needs.
    - **Compliance**: Easier to comply with stringent regulatory requirements regarding data sovereignty.
- **Disadvantages**:
    - **Cost**: Higher initial investment in hardware and infrastructure. Ongoing maintenance and upgrades can be costly.
    - **Scalability**: Scaling on-premise infrastructure can be challenging and time-consuming.
    - **Resource Management**: Requires dedicated IT staff to manage and maintain the infrastructure.

Cloud Deployment

- **Overview**: Cloud deployment involves hosting AI solutions on cloud platforms provided by vendors like AWS, Google Cloud, or Microsoft Azure.
- **Advantages**:
    - **Scalability**: Easily scalable to accommodate growing data and processing needs.
    - **Cost Efficiency**: Pay-as-you-go model reduces upfront costs and allows for cost-effective scaling.
    - **Managed Services**: Access to a wide range of managed services and tools that simplify AI deployment and management.
- **Disadvantages**:
    - **Data Privacy**: Potential concerns over data privacy and control when using third-party cloud services.
    - **Latency**: Network latency can be an issue for real-time applications, depending on the location of data centers.
    - **Compliance**: Ensuring compliance with regulations when data is stored and processed in the cloud.

Hybrid Solutions

- **Overview**: Hybrid deployment combines on-premise and cloud solutions, allowing organizations to leverage the benefits of both approaches.
- **Advantages**:

- o **Flexibility**: Balance between control and scalability. Critical data can be kept on-premise, while less sensitive workloads are moved to the cloud.
- o **Cost Management**: Optimize costs by using on-premise resources for predictable workloads and cloud for variable or peak loads.
- o **Business Continuity**: Enhanced business continuity and disaster recovery capabilities by leveraging both on-premise and cloud resources.
- **Disadvantages**:
  - o **Complexity**: Managing and integrating hybrid environments can be complex and require robust governance and orchestration.
  - o **Interoperability**: Ensuring seamless interoperability between on-premise and cloud components can be challenging.
  - o **Security**: Maintaining consistent security policies across on-premise and cloud environments.

Choosing the Right Strategy

- **Assessment**: Conduct a thorough assessment of the organization's needs, existing infrastructure, budget, and regulatory requirements.
- **Proof of Concept (PoC)**: Develop a PoC to evaluate the feasibility and performance of different deployment strategies.

- **Stakeholder Involvement**: Involve key stakeholders in the decision-making process to ensure alignment with business objectives and requirements.

7.3 Monitoring and Maintenance: Ensuring Ongoing Performance and Improvements

Introduction

After deploying AI solutions, continuous monitoring and maintenance are essential to ensure ongoing performance and drive continuous improvements. This section covers best practices for monitoring, maintaining, and improving AI systems.

Performance Monitoring

- **Key Metrics**: Identify and track key performance metrics to evaluate the effectiveness of AI models.
    - **Accuracy**: Measure the accuracy of predictions or classifications.
    - **Response Time**: Monitor the time taken to generate predictions.
    - **Resource Utilization**: Track CPU, memory, and storage usage to ensure efficient resource utilization.
- **Monitoring Tools**: Use monitoring tools and dashboards to visualize and track performance metrics.
    - **Prometheus and Grafana**: Open-source tools for monitoring and visualizing metrics.

- **Cloud Monitoring Services**: Utilize built-in monitoring services provided by cloud platforms (e.g., AWS CloudWatch, Google Cloud Monitoring).

Error Handling and Logging
- **Error Logs**: Maintain detailed logs of errors and exceptions encountered during model execution.
  - **Log Management**: Use log management tools like ELK Stack (Elasticsearch, Logstash, Kibana) or Splunk to aggregate and analyze logs.
- **Alerting**: Set up automated alerts to notify stakeholders of critical issues or performance degradation.
  - **Alerting Systems**: Implement alerting systems like PagerDuty or Opsgenie to manage and respond to alerts.

Regular Maintenance
- **Model Retraining**: Regularly retrain models with new data to maintain accuracy and relevance.
  - **Scheduled Retraining**: Establish a schedule for periodic retraining based on data availability and business needs.
- **Updating Dependencies**: Keep the software and libraries used in AI models up-to-date to ensure security and performance.
  - **Version Control**: Use version control systems like Git to manage and track changes to code and dependencies.

- **Scalability Testing**: Conduct scalability testing to ensure models can handle increased data volume and user load.
    - **Load Testing**: Use load testing tools like Apache JMeter or Locust to simulate high-traffic scenarios and evaluate performance.

Continuous Improvement

- **Feedback Loops**: Implement feedback loops to collect insights and feedback from end-users and stakeholders.
    - **User Feedback**: Gather user feedback through surveys, interviews, and usability testing.
    - **Performance Reviews**: Conduct regular performance reviews to identify areas for improvement.
- **A/B Testing**: Use A/B testing to compare different model versions and configurations to determine the best-performing solution.
    - **Experimental Design**: Design experiments to test different model variations and measure their impact on performance metrics.
- **Model Audits**: Perform periodic audits of AI models to ensure they remain aligned with business goals and ethical standards.
    - **Ethical Audits**: Evaluate models for fairness, bias, and compliance with ethical guidelines.
    - **Performance Audits**: Review model performance and identify opportunities for optimization and enhancement.

Conclusion

Integrating and deploying AI solutions effectively is crucial for maximizing their impact on business operations. By embedding AI into existing systems, choosing the right deployment strategy, and implementing robust monitoring and maintenance practices, organizations can ensure the ongoing success and improvement of their AI initiatives. This chapter has provided a comprehensive guide to these critical aspects, enabling businesses to harness the full potential of AI technology.

PROMPT - Write a thorough chapter 8 on Ethical and Legal Considerations, with subchapters on AI Ethics: Bias, transparency, accountability; Regulatory Compliance: GDPR, CCPA, and other regulations; and Corporate Responsibility: Ensuring ethical use of AI.

Chapter 8: Ethical and Legal Considerations

As AI technology becomes increasingly integrated into business operations and decision-making processes, it is crucial to address the ethical and legal considerations that come with its use. This chapter explores the importance of AI ethics, the regulatory landscape, and corporate responsibility in ensuring the ethical deployment and use of AI.

8.1 AI Ethics: Bias, Transparency, Accountability

Introduction
AI ethics is a framework that guides the development and deployment of AI technologies in a manner that is fair, transparent, and accountable. Addressing ethical concerns is essential to maintain public trust and ensure that AI systems are used responsibly.

Bias in AI
- **Understanding Bias**: Bias in AI occurs when the outcomes of an AI system unfairly favor certain groups over others. This can happen due to biased training data, flawed algorithms, or systemic inequalities.
    - **Types of Bias**:
        - **Data Bias**: Occurs when the training data is not representative of the population.

- **Algorithmic Bias**: Arises from the design of the algorithms themselves.
- **Social Bias**: Reflects existing societal prejudices and inequalities.
- **Mitigating Bias**:
    o **Diverse Data Collection**: Ensure that training data is diverse and representative of all relevant groups.
    o **Bias Detection Tools**: Use tools and techniques to detect and measure bias in AI models.
    o **Fairness Metrics**: Implement fairness metrics to evaluate the impact of AI systems on different groups.
    o **Regular Audits**: Conduct regular audits of AI models to identify and mitigate bias.

Transparency

- **Importance of Transparency**: Transparency involves making the workings of AI systems understandable to stakeholders, including how decisions are made and the data used.
    o **Explainable AI (XAI)**: Develop AI models that can explain their reasoning and decisions in a human-understandable manner.
    o **Documentation**: Maintain detailed documentation of AI model development, including data sources, algorithms used, and decision-making processes.

- o **Communication**: Clearly communicate the capabilities and limitations of AI systems to users and stakeholders.

Accountability

- **Responsibility for AI Outcomes**: Accountability ensures that individuals and organizations are responsible for the outcomes of AI systems.
    - o **Clear Governance Structures**: Establish governance structures that define roles and responsibilities for AI development and deployment.
    - o **Ethical Guidelines**: Develop and adhere to ethical guidelines for AI use, including principles of fairness, transparency, and accountability.
    - o **Liability and Recourse**: Define processes for addressing and rectifying issues that arise from AI systems, including legal liabilities and recourse for affected parties.

8.2 Regulatory Compliance: GDPR, CCPA, and Other Regulations

Introduction

Compliance with regulations is critical for organizations using AI, as failure to adhere to legal standards can result in significant penalties and reputational damage. This section covers key regulations, including GDPR, CCPA, and other relevant laws.

General Data Protection Regulation (GDPR)
- **Overview**: GDPR is a comprehensive data protection regulation implemented by the European Union to safeguard personal data and privacy.
    - **Key Provisions**:
        - **Consent**: Obtain explicit consent from individuals before collecting and processing their personal data.
        - **Data Subject Rights**: Respect the rights of data subjects, including the right to access, rectify, and erase their data.
        - **Data Protection Officer (DPO)**: Appoint a DPO to oversee compliance with GDPR.
        - **Data Breach Notification**: Notify authorities and affected individuals of data breaches within 72 hours.
- **Implications for AI**:
    - **Data Minimization**: Limit the amount of personal data collected and processed by AI systems.
    - **Transparency**: Inform individuals about how their data is used by AI systems.
    - **Algorithmic Decision-Making**: Provide explanations for decisions made by AI systems that affect individuals.

California Consumer Privacy Act (CCPA)

- **Overview**: CCPA is a data privacy law enacted in California to enhance privacy rights and consumer protection.
    - **Key Provisions**:
        - **Right to Know**: Allow consumers to know what personal data is being collected and how it is used.
        - **Right to Delete**: Enable consumers to request the deletion of their personal data.
        - **Right to Opt-Out**: Provide consumers with the option to opt-out of the sale of their personal data.
        - **Non-Discrimination**: Prohibit discrimination against consumers who exercise their privacy rights.
- **Implications for AI**:
    - **Data Access and Deletion**: Implement mechanisms to allow consumers to access and delete their data from AI systems.
    - **Opt-Out Mechanisms**: Provide clear options for consumers to opt-out of data collection and processing.
    - **Transparency**: Clearly communicate data practices to consumers, including the use of AI.

Other Relevant Regulations

- **Health Insurance Portability and Accountability Act (HIPAA)**: U.S. regulation that protects the privacy and security of health information. AI systems handling health data must comply with HIPAA standards.
- **Fair Credit Reporting Act (FCRA)**: U.S. law that regulates the collection and use of consumer credit information. AI systems used in credit scoring and reporting must adhere to FCRA requirements.
- **Personal Data Protection Bill (India)**: Proposed legislation in India aimed at protecting personal data and establishing data protection authorities. AI systems operating in India must comply with this regulation.

Compliance Strategies

- **Data Protection Impact Assessments (DPIAs)**: Conduct DPIAs to assess and mitigate risks associated with AI data processing activities.
- **Training and Awareness**: Provide training and raise awareness among employees about regulatory requirements and best practices.
- **Legal Counsel**: Engage legal counsel to navigate complex regulatory landscapes and ensure compliance.

8.3 Corporate Responsibility: Ensuring Ethical Use of AI

Introduction
Corporate responsibility in AI involves not only adhering to ethical and legal standards but also actively promoting the responsible and beneficial use of AI within the organization and society at large.

Developing an Ethical AI Framework

- **Ethical Principles**: Establish a set of ethical principles that guide AI development and deployment, including fairness, accountability, transparency, and respect for privacy.
- **Ethics Committees**: Form ethics committees or boards to oversee AI projects and ensure they align with the organization's ethical principles.
- **Stakeholder Engagement**: Involve stakeholders, including employees, customers, and the community, in discussions about the ethical implications of AI.

Promoting Diversity and Inclusion

- **Diverse Teams**: Build diverse and inclusive teams to develop AI systems, ensuring a variety of perspectives and reducing the risk of bias.
- **Inclusive Data Practices**: Ensure that data collection and processing practices consider and respect the diversity of the population.

- **Community Outreach**: Engage with communities to understand their concerns and perspectives on AI and incorporate their feedback into AI development.

Ethical AI Usage Policies

- **Use Case Evaluation**: Carefully evaluate AI use cases to ensure they align with ethical standards and do not cause harm.
- **Transparency Policies**: Implement policies that promote transparency in AI systems, including clear communication about how AI is used and how decisions are made.
- **Accountability Measures**: Establish accountability measures to address and rectify any negative impacts of AI systems.

Corporate Social Responsibility (CSR) in AI

- **Ethical AI Initiatives**: Invest in initiatives that promote ethical AI research and development, such as partnerships with academic institutions and participation in industry standards organizations.
- **Public Commitments**: Make public commitments to ethical AI practices, such as signing onto AI ethics pledges or participating in responsible AI consortia.
- **Impact Assessments**: Regularly assess the social and environmental impact of AI systems and take steps to mitigate any negative effects.

Building Trust and Transparency

- **Open Communication**: Maintain open lines of communication with stakeholders about AI initiatives, including potential risks and benefits.
- **Public Reporting**: Publish regular reports on the organization's AI activities, including performance metrics, ethical considerations, and compliance efforts.
- **Community Engagement**: Actively engage with the community to build trust and address concerns about AI technologies.

Conclusion

Ethical and legal considerations are critical to the successful and responsible implementation of AI technologies. By addressing issues of bias, transparency, and accountability, complying with relevant regulations, and embracing corporate responsibility, organizations can ensure that their AI initiatives are ethical, legal, and beneficial to all stakeholders. This chapter provides a comprehensive framework for navigating these complex issues and promoting the ethical use of AI in business.

PROMPT - Dive deep, thoroughly, and abundant into a chapter 9: Managing Change, developing subchapters on Change Management: Strategies for smooth transitions; Training and Support: Educating staff and stakeholders; and Measuring Success: KPIs and metrics for AI projects.

Chapter 9: Managing Change

Successfully implementing AI in business requires more than just technological advancements; it necessitates a comprehensive change management strategy. This chapter explores the strategies for managing change, training and supporting staff, and measuring the success of AI projects through key performance indicators (KPIs) and metrics.

9.1 Change Management: Strategies for Smooth Transitions

Introduction

Change management is a structured approach to transitioning individuals, teams, and organizations from a current state to a desired future state. Effective change management ensures that the implementation of AI technologies is accepted and utilized effectively across the organization.

Understanding the Need for Change

- **Assessing Readiness**: Evaluate the organizationâ€™s readiness for change by understanding its current culture, processes, and technology landscape.
- **Identifying Drivers**: Identify the key drivers for AI adoption, such as improving efficiency, gaining competitive advantage, or enhancing customer experience.

- **Stakeholder Analysis**: Conduct a stakeholder analysis to identify all parties affected by the AI implementation and their potential concerns.

Developing a Change Management Strategy

- **Vision and Objectives**: Clearly define the vision and objectives of the AI initiative. Communicate how AI will align with the organization's goals and benefit stakeholders.
- **Leadership and Sponsorship**: Secure commitment from top leadership to champion the AI initiative. Leaders should visibly support the change and address any resistance.
- **Change Management Team**: Form a dedicated change management team responsible for planning, executing, and monitoring change initiatives.

Communication Plan

- **Transparent Communication**: Maintain open and transparent communication throughout the AI implementation process. Regularly update stakeholders on progress, challenges, and successes.
- **Feedback Mechanisms**: Establish channels for employees to provide feedback, ask questions, and express concerns. Addressing these promptly can reduce resistance and build trust.
- **Messaging**: Craft clear and consistent messaging that explains the reasons for the change, the benefits of AI, and how it will impact various roles and processes.

Managing Resistance

- **Understanding Resistance**: Recognize that resistance to change is natural. Identify the sources of resistance, whether they stem from fear of job loss, lack of understanding, or discomfort with new technologies.
- **Addressing Concerns**: Address concerns through targeted communication, education, and involvement in the change process. Show empathy and provide support to ease the transition.
- **Involvement and Participation**: Involve employees in the change process by seeking their input and involving them in decision-making. This can increase buy-in and reduce resistance.

Implementing Change

- **Pilot Programs**: Start with pilot programs to test AI solutions on a smaller scale. Use the insights gained to refine the implementation plan and demonstrate success.
- **Phased Rollout**: Consider a phased rollout of AI solutions to manage the transition gradually. This approach allows for adjustments based on feedback and minimizes disruptions.
- **Support Structures**: Establish support structures, such as help desks, training sessions, and user guides, to assist employees in adapting to new AI tools and processes.

9.2 Training and Support: Educating Staff and Stakeholders

Introduction
Training and support are critical components of a successful AI implementation. Educating staff and stakeholders about AI technologies, their applications, and how to use them effectively ensures a smooth transition and maximizes the benefits of AI.

Identifying Training Needs

- **Skills Assessment**: Conduct a skills assessment to identify the current competencies of employees and the skills required for AI adoption.
- **Role-Specific Training**: Tailor training programs to the specific needs of different roles within the organization, such as data scientists, IT staff, business analysts, and end-users.

Developing a Training Program

- **Training Objectives**: Define clear training objectives aligned with the goals of the AI initiative. Objectives should focus on building both technical and soft skills.
- **Training Content**: Develop comprehensive training content covering AI fundamentals, specific AI tools and technologies, data literacy, and practical applications.
    - **Technical Training**: Provide in-depth training on AI models, algorithms, and programming languages for technical staff.

- - **Business Training**: Focus on how AI can solve business problems, improve processes, and drive value for non-technical staff.
- **Training Methods**: Utilize a variety of training methods to cater to different learning styles and preferences.
  - **Workshops and Seminars**: Conduct interactive workshops and seminars to provide hands-on learning experiences.
  - **Online Courses and Webinars**: Offer flexible online courses and webinars for remote learning.
  - **Self-Paced Learning**: Provide access to self-paced learning resources, such as e-learning modules, videos, and reading materials.

Ongoing Support

- **Help Desks and Support Teams**: Establish help desks and support teams to provide immediate assistance and resolve issues encountered by employees.
- **Mentorship and Coaching**: Implement mentorship and coaching programs to provide personalized support and guidance.
- **Community of Practice**: Create communities of practice where employees can share knowledge, best practices, and experiences related to AI.

Assessing Training Effectiveness

- **Feedback and Evaluation**: Collect feedback from participants to evaluate the effectiveness of training

programs. Use surveys, quizzes, and assessments to measure learning outcomes.
- **Continuous Improvement**: Continuously refine training programs based on feedback and changing needs. Stay updated with the latest developments in AI to ensure training remains relevant.

9.3 Measuring Success: KPIs and Metrics for AI Projects

Introduction
Measuring the success of AI projects is crucial to demonstrate their value, identify areas for improvement, and guide future initiatives. This section outlines key performance indicators (KPIs) and metrics to evaluate the effectiveness and impact of AI solutions.

Defining Success Criteria

- **Align with Objectives**: Define success criteria that align with the objectives of the AI initiative. Success criteria should be specific, measurable, achievable, relevant, and time-bound (SMART).
- **Stakeholder Involvement**: Involve stakeholders in defining success criteria to ensure they reflect the needs and expectations of the organization.

Key Performance Indicators (KPIs)
- **Operational Efficiency**:
    - **Processing Time**: Measure the time taken to complete tasks or processes before and after AI implementation.
    - **Cost Savings**: Calculate cost savings achieved through automation and improved efficiency.
    - **Resource Utilization**: Track the utilization of resources, such as manpower and computational resources, before and after AI implementation.
- **Accuracy and Performance**:
    - **Model Accuracy**: Evaluate the accuracy of AI models using metrics such as precision, recall, F1 score, and ROC-AUC.
    - **Error Rates**: Measure the reduction in error rates or false positives/negatives achieved by AI models.
- **Business Impact**:
    - **Revenue Growth**: Assess the impact of AI on revenue growth, such as increased sales or reduced churn rates.
    - **Customer Satisfaction**: Measure changes in customer satisfaction and engagement through surveys and feedback.
- **Adoption and Usage**:
    - **User Adoption**: Track the adoption rate of AI tools and technologies among employees.
    - **Usage Metrics**: Monitor usage metrics, such as the number of users, frequency of use, and duration of use.

- **Innovation and Improvement**:
  - **New Capabilities**: Evaluate the introduction of new capabilities or services enabled by AI.
  - **Continuous Improvement**: Measure the impact of AI on continuous improvement initiatives, such as process optimization and innovation.

Data Collection and Analysis

- **Data Sources**: Identify the data sources needed to track KPIs and metrics, such as system logs, performance reports, and user feedback.
- **Data Analysis Tools**: Use data analysis tools and dashboards to visualize and analyze KPI data. Tools like Tableau, Power BI, or custom-built dashboards can provide real-time insights.
- **Regular Reporting**: Establish a regular reporting schedule to review KPI data with stakeholders and make data-driven decisions.

Continuous Monitoring and Improvement

- **Performance Reviews**: Conduct regular performance reviews to assess the progress of AI projects and identify areas for improvement.
- **Agile Methodologies**: Apply agile methodologies to iterate and improve AI solutions based on feedback and performance data.

- **Benchmarking**: Benchmark AI performance against industry standards and best practices to identify opportunities for enhancement.

Conclusion

Managing change effectively is critical for the successful implementation of AI in business. By developing comprehensive change management strategies, providing robust training and support, and measuring success through relevant KPIs and metrics, organizations can ensure that AI initiatives deliver tangible value and drive continuous improvement. This chapter provides a detailed framework for navigating the complexities of change management in the context of AI adoption.

PROMPT - Write a thoughtful and reasoned chapter 10 on Future Trends in AI, developing subchapters on Emerging Technologies: Quantum computing, edge AI; AI and Society: Impact on jobs, economy, and culture; and Preparing for the Future: Staying ahead in the AI landscape.

Chapter 10: Future Trends in AI

As AI continues to evolve, it brings with it new possibilities and challenges. This chapter explores the future trends in AI, focusing on emerging technologies, the societal impact of AI, and strategies for staying ahead in the AI landscape.

10.1 Emerging Technologies: Quantum Computing, Edge AI

Introduction
Emerging technologies like quantum computing and edge AI are poised to revolutionize the capabilities and applications of AI. Understanding these technologies and their potential impact is crucial for businesses looking to remain competitive.

Quantum Computing
- **Overview of Quantum Computing**: Quantum computing leverages the principles of quantum mechanics to perform computations far more efficiently than classical computers. Quantum bits, or qubits, can exist in multiple states simultaneously, enabling massive parallelism and complex problem-solving capabilities.
    - **Speed and Power**: Quantum computers can solve problems that are currently intractable for classical computers, such as complex optimization problems, molecular simulations, and cryptographic challenges.

- - - o **Applications in AI**: Quantum computing can enhance AI in various ways:
      - **Optimization**: Quantum algorithms can optimize AI models and processes more effectively.
      - **Machine Learning**: Quantum machine learning algorithms can process and analyze large datasets at unprecedented speeds.
      - **Cryptography**: Quantum computing can improve data security, a critical aspect of AI systems.
  - **Challenges and Considerations**:
    - o **Technological Maturity**: Quantum computing is still in its early stages, and practical, scalable quantum computers are not yet widely available.
    - o **Integration**: Integrating quantum computing with existing AI systems and infrastructure poses technical and logistical challenges.

Edge AI

- **Overview of Edge AI**: Edge AI involves deploying AI algorithms on edge devices (e.g., smartphones, IoT devices) rather than relying solely on centralized cloud servers. This approach enables real-time data processing and decision-making closer to the data source.
  - o **Latency and Bandwidth**: By processing data locally, edge AI reduces latency and bandwidth

usage, leading to faster and more efficient operations.
- o **Privacy and Security**: Edge AI enhances data privacy and security by minimizing the need to transmit sensitive data to centralized servers.
- **Applications in AI**:
  - o **Smart Devices**: Edge AI powers intelligent features in smartphones, wearables, and home automation systems.
  - o **Industrial IoT**: In manufacturing and logistics, edge AI enables real-time monitoring, predictive maintenance, and autonomous operations.
  - o **Healthcare**: Edge AI supports remote health monitoring, diagnostics, and personalized treatments through smart medical devices.
- **Challenges and Considerations**:
  - o **Hardware Constraints**: Edge devices have limited computational resources compared to cloud servers, requiring efficient algorithms and lightweight models.
  - o **Deployment and Management**: Managing and updating AI models across a distributed network of edge devices can be complex.

10.2 AI and Society: Impact on Jobs, Economy, and Culture

Introduction
AI has profound implications for society, affecting jobs, the economy, and culture. Understanding these impacts helps businesses and policymakers navigate the changes and leverage AI for positive outcomes.

Impact on Jobs
- **Automation and Job Displacement**: AI and automation are expected to transform the job market by automating routine and repetitive tasks. This can lead to job displacement in certain sectors, particularly those involving manual labor and administrative work.
    - **Reskilling and Upskilling**: To mitigate job displacement, there is a growing need for reskilling and upskilling programs that prepare the workforce for new roles created by AI. Emphasis on digital literacy, critical thinking, and complex problem-solving skills is essential.
    - **New Job Opportunities**: AI also creates new job opportunities in areas such as AI development, data science, cybersecurity, and AI ethics. These roles require specialized skills and offer growth potential.
- **Changing Nature of Work**: The integration of AI into the workplace is changing how work is performed.
    - **Human-AI Collaboration**: AI is augmenting human capabilities, enabling more efficient and innovative work processes. Collaborative AI

systems assist humans in decision-making, creativity, and problem-solving.
- **Flexible Work Arrangements**: AI-powered tools facilitate remote work, virtual collaboration, and flexible work arrangements, contributing to a more dynamic and adaptable workforce.

Impact on the Economy
- **Productivity and Growth**: AI has the potential to significantly boost productivity and economic growth by optimizing processes, reducing costs, and driving innovation. Industries such as manufacturing, healthcare, finance, and retail are experiencing transformative impacts from AI.
    - **Economic Disparities**: While AI-driven growth offers substantial benefits, it can also exacerbate economic disparities. Organizations and regions that successfully adopt AI may gain a competitive edge, while those that lag behind could face economic challenges.
- **Market Dynamics**: AI is reshaping market dynamics by creating new business models and disrupting traditional industries.
    - **Platform Economies**: AI-driven platforms are becoming central to various sectors, from e-commerce and ride-sharing to digital content and financial services.
    - **Startups and Innovation**: AI is fueling the growth of startups and innovation ecosystems,

driving advancements in technology and creating new market opportunities.

Impact on Culture
- **Societal Changes**: AI is influencing societal norms and behaviors in multiple ways.
    - **Digital Interaction**: AI-powered virtual assistants, chatbots, and social media algorithms are changing how people interact with technology and each other.
    - **Ethical Considerations**: The ethical implications of AI, such as privacy, bias, and accountability, are becoming central to societal debates. Public awareness and discourse on these issues are crucial for shaping ethical AI practices.
- **Cultural Adaptation**: As AI becomes more integrated into daily life, cultural adaptation is necessary.
    - **Education and Awareness**: Promoting education and awareness about AI and its implications helps society adapt to changes and make informed decisions.
    - **Cultural Diversity**: Ensuring that AI systems respect and reflect cultural diversity is important for their acceptance and effectiveness across different communities.

10.3 Preparing for the Future: Staying Ahead in the AI Landscape

Introduction
Staying ahead in the rapidly evolving AI landscape requires proactive strategies, continuous learning, and adaptability. This section outlines key strategies for preparing for the future of AI.

Continuous Learning and Adaptation
- **Lifelong Learning**: Emphasize lifelong learning and continuous professional development to keep pace with AI advancements. Encourage employees to acquire new skills and stay updated with the latest trends.
    - **Online Courses and Certifications**: Leverage online courses, certifications, and training programs to build AI-related skills.
    - **Workshops and Seminars**: Participate in workshops, seminars, and conferences to gain insights from industry experts and network with peers.
- **Innovation Culture**: Foster a culture of innovation within the organization.
    - **Encouraging Experimentation**: Encourage experimentation and pilot projects to explore new AI applications and technologies.
    - **Supporting Creativity**: Support creative problem-solving and collaboration to drive AI-driven innovation.

Strategic Partnerships and Collaborations
- **Industry Partnerships**: Form strategic partnerships with technology providers, research institutions, and other organizations to leverage external expertise and resources.
  - **Joint Ventures**: Engage in joint ventures and collaborative projects to accelerate AI development and deployment.
  - **Knowledge Sharing**: Participate in industry consortia and knowledge-sharing platforms to stay informed about best practices and emerging trends.
- **Research and Development (R&D)**: Invest in R&D to explore new AI technologies and applications.
  - **Internal R&D Teams**: Establish internal R&D teams dedicated to AI research and innovation.
  - **Collaboration with Academia**: Collaborate with academic institutions to access cutting-edge research and talent.

Agility and Flexibility
- **Agile Methodologies**: Adopt agile methodologies to quickly respond to changes and iteratively improve AI solutions.
  - **Iterative Development**: Implement iterative development processes to refine AI models and applications based on feedback and performance data.
  - **Cross-Functional Teams**: Form cross-functional teams to integrate diverse perspectives and expertise into AI projects.

- **Scalable Infrastructure**: Build a scalable and flexible infrastructure that can accommodate evolving AI technologies and growing data needs.
  - **Cloud Solutions**: Leverage cloud solutions to ensure scalability, flexibility, and cost-effectiveness.
  - **Edge Computing**: Integrate edge computing capabilities to support real-time data processing and decision-making.

Ethical and Responsible AI

- **Ethical Guidelines**: Develop and adhere to ethical guidelines for AI development and deployment.
  - **Transparency and Accountability**: Ensure transparency in AI systems and establish mechanisms for accountability.
  - **Bias Mitigation**: Implement strategies to detect and mitigate bias in AI models and datasets.
- **Stakeholder Engagement**: Engage stakeholders in discussions about the ethical implications of AI.
  - **Community Involvement**: Involve communities in AI decision-making processes to ensure diverse perspectives and address concerns.
  - **Public Communication**: Communicate openly about AI initiatives, their benefits, and potential risks.

Future-Proofing Strategies

- **Scenario Planning**: Conduct scenario planning to anticipate potential future developments and prepare for different outcomes.

- o **Risk Management**: Identify and mitigate risks associated with AI adoption, including technological, regulatory, and ethical risks.
- o **Flexibility and Adaptability**: Cultivate flexibility and adaptability to navigate the dynamic AI landscape.
- **Sustainable AI Practices**: Promote sustainable AI practices that consider environmental, social, and economic impacts.
  - o **Energy Efficiency**: Develop energy-efficient AI solutions to reduce the environmental footprint.
  - o **Inclusive AI**: Ensure that AI benefits are distributed equitably and that AI systems are inclusive and accessible.

Conclusion

The future of AI holds immense promise, driven by emerging technologies like quantum computing and edge AI, and shaped by its profound impact.

PROMPT - Go over the whole conversation in this project and write a thorough and deep conclusion chapter that is relevant and avoid being repetitive nor redundant, encouraging readers to keep learning and moving forward into AI adoption in productive domains.

Conclusion

The journey of implementing AI in business is both transformative and complex. This book has covered a wide range of topics to equip you with the knowledge and tools necessary to navigate this journey successfully. As we conclude, it's crucial to reflect on the key lessons learned and provide a clear path forward for continued learning and adaptation in the ever-evolving AI landscape.

Key Takeaways

Chapter 1: Introduction to AI in Business We began by understanding what AI is, its history, and its relevance to modern business. We explored the various types of AI, including machine learning, natural language processing, computer vision, and robotics, and highlighted their applications across different industries.

Chapter 2: Case Studies of Successful AI Implementation Through detailed case studies, we examined how various industries have successfully implemented AI, from finance and healthcare to retail and manufacturing. These examples provided practical insights and highlighted key strategies and lessons learned that can be applied in similar contexts.

Chapter 3: Setting AI Objectives and Roadmap We emphasized the importance of aligning AI initiatives with business goals and provided frameworks for setting clear objectives and developing a strategic AI roadmap. This chapter underscored the need for careful planning and execution to ensure AI projects deliver tangible business value.

Chapter 4: Data Management Data is the foundation of AI. We discussed the critical aspects of data management, including data collection methods, ensuring data quality, and implementing robust data governance policies. These elements are essential for building reliable and effective AI systems.

Chapter 5: Choosing the Right AI Solutions Choosing the right AI solutions is a crucial step. We explored different AI technologies like natural language processing, computer vision, and predictive analytics. Additionally, we discussed the pros and cons of building AI solutions in-house versus purchasing third-party solutions and provided criteria for evaluating AI vendors.

Chapter 6: Developing AI Models This chapter delved into the core of AI development, covering the basics of machine learning, including supervised, unsupervised, and reinforcement learning. We also discussed the process of model training, data preparation, validation, and testing, as well as the tools and frameworks such as TensorFlow, PyTorch, and Scikit-Learn.

Chapter 7: Integration and Deployment We examined the challenges and strategies for integrating AI into existing systems, deploying AI solutions on-premise, in the cloud, or through hybrid approaches. Additionally, we highlighted the importance of monitoring and maintenance to ensure ongoing performance and continuous improvements.

Chapter 8: Ethical and Legal Considerations Ethics and compliance are paramount in AI adoption. We discussed critical ethical issues such as bias, transparency, and accountability, and reviewed regulatory frameworks like GDPR and CCPA. Ensuring ethical use of AI is not only a legal requirement but also essential for building trust with stakeholders.

Chapter 9: Managing Change Implementing AI involves significant change management. This chapter provided strategies for managing transitions smoothly, training and supporting staff and stakeholders, and measuring the success of AI projects using relevant KPIs and metrics.

Chapter 10: Future Trends in AI Looking ahead, we explored emerging technologies like quantum computing and edge AI, and their potential impacts. We also examined the broader societal implications of AI, including its effects on jobs, the economy, and culture, and provided strategies for staying ahead in the AI landscape.

Moving Forward: Embrace Continuous Learning and Adaptation

Lifelong Learning AI is a rapidly evolving field, and staying updated with the latest developments is crucial. Encourage continuous professional development through online courses, certifications, workshops, and industry conferences. Building a culture of lifelong learning within your organization will ensure that your team remains at the forefront of AI innovation.

Foster Collaboration and Inclusivity Successful AI implementation requires collaboration across various functions and levels of the organization. Promote an inclusive environment where diverse perspectives are valued and foster cross-functional teams to integrate different expertise into AI projects. This approach enhances creativity and helps build more robust and fair AI systems.

Prioritize Ethical AI Ethical considerations must be at the heart of AI development and deployment. Establish clear ethical guidelines, ensure transparency, and build accountability mechanisms into your AI systems. Engage with stakeholders to discuss ethical implications and prioritize the development of AI solutions that are fair, unbiased, and beneficial to society.

Leverage Emerging Technologies Stay informed about emerging technologies such as quantum computing and edge AI. While these technologies are still maturing, they hold significant potential to revolutionize AI capabilities. Being early adopters can provide a competitive edge and position your organization at the cutting edge of AI advancements.

Build Adaptability and Resilience The AI landscape is dynamic, and adaptability is key to thriving amidst changes. Develop flexible AI strategies that can evolve with technological advancements and market conditions. Invest in scalable infrastructure and foster a culture of agility to quickly respond to new opportunities and challenges.

Strategic Partnerships and Innovation Form strategic partnerships with technology providers, research institutions, and industry consortia to leverage external expertise and resources. Engage in joint ventures and collaborative projects to accelerate AI innovation. Promote a culture of experimentation and support creative problem-solving to drive continuous improvement.

Future-Proofing and Sustainability Conduct scenario planning to anticipate future developments and mitigate risks associated with AI adoption. Emphasize sustainable AI practices that consider environmental, social, and economic impacts. Develop energy-efficient AI solutions and ensure that AI benefits are distributed equitably across society.

Final Thoughts

The journey of AI adoption is ongoing and requires a commitment to continuous learning, collaboration, and ethical practices. AI has the power to transform businesses and society, driving innovation, efficiency, and growth. By staying informed, fostering a culture of innovation, and prioritizing ethical considerations, you can harness the full potential of AI and navigate the complexities of its implementation effectively.

As you move forward, embrace the opportunities that AI presents, remain adaptable to change, and commit to responsible AI practices. The future of AI is bright, and with the right strategies and mindset, your organization can lead the way in this transformative era, creating value and making a positive impact on the world.

Keep learning, stay curious, and continue to innovate. The journey of AI is just beginning, and the possibilities are endless.

PROMPT - Write a comprehensive glossary of the book developed in this project.

Glossary

AI (Artificial Intelligence): A branch of computer science that focuses on creating systems capable of performing tasks that typically require human intelligence, such as visual perception, speech recognition, decision-making, and language translation.

Algorithm: A set of rules or instructions given to an AI system to help it learn and make decisions.

Bias: Prejudices or systematic errors in AI systems that can lead to unfair or inaccurate outcomes.

Big Data: Large and complex data sets that traditional data processing software cannot handle efficiently. Big data is often used in AI to train models.

Cloud Computing: The delivery of computing services, including storage and processing power, over the internet, allowing for scalable and flexible AI deployment.

Computer Vision: A field of AI that enables machines to interpret and make decisions based on visual data from the world.

Data Collection: The process of gathering and measuring information on variables of interest in a systematic fashion.

Data Governance: The overall management of data availability, usability, integrity, and security within an organization, ensuring data quality and compliance with regulations.

Data Quality: The condition of a data set, characterized by its accuracy, completeness, reliability, and relevance.

Deep Learning: A subset of machine learning involving neural networks with many layers, which can model complex patterns in data.

Edge AI: AI computation performed locally on hardware devices rather than in a centralized data center or cloud.

Ethics in AI: The study and practice of ensuring AI systems operate in a fair, transparent, and accountable manner, minimizing biases and preventing harm.

GDPR (General Data Protection Regulation): A regulation in EU law on data protection and privacy, affecting how organizations collect and process personal data.

Hybrid Solutions: AI deployment strategies that combine both on-premise and cloud-based approaches.

In-House Development: Creating AI solutions using an organization's internal resources and expertise.

KPI (Key Performance Indicator): A measurable value that indicates how effectively an organization is achieving key business objectives.

Machine Learning: A type of AI that allows software applications to become more accurate in predicting outcomes without being explicitly programmed to do so. Machine learning algorithms use historical data as input to predict new output values.

Model Training: The process of teaching an AI model to make predictions or decisions by feeding it data and allowing it to learn patterns.

Natural Language Processing (NLP): A field of AI focused on the interaction between computers and humans through natural language, enabling machines to understand, interpret, and generate human language.

On-Premise Deployment: AI solutions hosted and managed within an organization's own infrastructure rather than on the cloud.

Predictive Analytics: A type of data analysis that uses statistical algorithms and machine learning techniques to identify the likelihood of future outcomes based on historical data.

Quantum Computing: An advanced computing technology that leverages the principles of quantum mechanics to perform calculations at speeds significantly faster than traditional computers.

Reinforcement Learning: A type of machine learning where an agent learns to make decisions by taking actions in an environment to achieve maximum cumulative reward.

Scikit-Learn: An open-source machine learning library for the Python programming language, providing simple and efficient tools for data mining and data analysis.

Supervised Learning: A type of machine learning where the model is trained on labeled data, meaning that each training example is paired with an output label.

TensorFlow: An open-source software library for dataflow and differentiable programming across a range of tasks, widely used for machine learning applications such as neural networks.

Third-Party Solutions: AI solutions developed by external vendors and integrated into an organization's existing systems.

Training Data: The data used to train an AI model, helping it learn patterns and make accurate predictions or decisions.

Transparency in AI: The practice of making AI systems and their decision-making processes understandable and interpretable by humans.

Unsupervised Learning: A type of machine learning where the model is trained on unlabeled data and must find patterns and relationships within the data on its own.

Validation: The process of evaluating a trained AI model on a separate data set to ensure it performs well and generalizes to new, unseen data.

Vendor Evaluation: The process of assessing and selecting third-party AI solution providers based on various criteria such as performance, reliability, and cost.

This glossary provides a comprehensive overview of the key terms and concepts discussed throughout the book. Understanding these terms will help you navigate the complex landscape of AI and implement effective AI solutions in your business.

PROMPT - Provide a thorough and comprehensive list of resources to learn about implementing AI in business, including resources for every chapter in the book developed in this conversation.

[...Resources...]

Implementing AI in business requires a multifaceted understanding of various concepts, tools, and strategies. Below is a comprehensive list of resources tailored to each chapter in this book, designed to help you deepen your knowledge and effectively leverage AI in your organization.

Chapter 1: Understanding AI
Books:

- "Artificial Intelligence: A Guide for Thinking Humans" by Melanie Mitchell
- "Artificial Intelligence: A Modern Approach" by Stuart Russell and Peter Norvig

Online Courses:

- "AI For Everyone" by Andrew Ng (Coursera)
- "Introduction to Artificial Intelligence (AI)" by IBM (Coursera)

Websites:

- AI Trends (https://www.aitrends.com/)
- AI News (https://ainews.site/)

Chapter 2: The Business Case for AI
Books:

- "Prediction Machines: The Simple Economics of Artificial Intelligence" by Ajay Agrawal, Joshua Gans, and Avi Goldfarb
- "Artificial Intelligence in Practice: How 50 Successful Companies Used AI and Machine Learning to Solve Problems" by Bernard Marr

Online Courses:

- "AI for Business Leaders" by Udacity
- "AI in Business" by Wharton Online (Coursera)

Websites:

- McKinsey on AI (https://www.mckinsey.com/business-functions/mckinsey-analytics/our-insights)
- Deloitte Insights on AI (https://www2.deloitte.com/us/en/insights/focus/cognitive-technologies.html)

Chapter 3: Setting AI Objectives

Books:

- "Competing in the Age of AI: Strategy and Leadership When Algorithms and Networks Run the World" by Marco Iansiti and Karim R. Lakhani
- "Human + Machine: Reimagining Work in the Age of AI" by Paul R. Daugherty and H. James Wilson

Online Courses:

- "AI Strategy and Roadmap: From Planning to Implementation" by the University of Toronto (Coursera)
- "AI for Business Transformation" by INSEAD (Coursera)

Websites:

- Harvard Business Review on AI Strategy (https://hbr.org/topic/artificial-intelligence)
- MIT Sloan Management Review on AI (https://sloanreview.mit.edu/ai/)

Chapter 4: Data Management
Books:

- "Data Management for Researchers: Organize, Maintain and Share Your Data for Research Success" by Kristin Briney
- "Data Governance: How to Design, Deploy, and Sustain an Effective Data Governance Program" by John Ladley

Online Courses:

- "Data Management and Visualization" by Wesleyan University (Coursera)
- "Data Governance and Privacy for Professionals" by Udacity

Websites:

- Data Management Association International (https://www.dama.org/)
- The Open Group: Data Management (https://www.opengroup.org/subjectareas/data-management)

Chapter 5: Choosing the Right AI Solutions
Books:

- "Machine Learning Yearning" by Andrew Ng (Available for free online)
- "Practical AI for Business Leaders" by Dr. Eric Siegel

Online Courses:

- "AI Product Management" by Udacity
- "How to Win with Machine Learning" by Andrew Ng (deeplearning.ai)

Websites:

- Gartner's AI Vendor Guide (https://www.gartner.com/en/information-technology)
- Forrester's AI Insights (https://go.forrester.com/blogs/category/artificial-intelligence/)

Chapter 6: Developing AI Models

Books:

- "Hands-On Machine Learning with Scikit-Learn, Keras, and TensorFlow" by Aurélien Géron
- "Deep Learning" by Ian Goodfellow, Yoshua Bengio, and Aaron Courville

Online Courses:

- "Deep Learning Specialization" by Andrew Ng (Coursera)
- "Machine Learning" by Stanford University (Coursera)

Websites:

- TensorFlow (https://www.tensorflow.org/)
- PyTorch (https://pytorch.org/)

Chapter 7: Integration and Deployment

Books:

- "Building Machine Learning Powered Applications: Going from Idea to Product" by Emmanuel Ameisen
- "Architects of Intelligence: The Truth About AI from the People Building It" by Martin Ford

Online Courses:

- "Deploying Machine Learning Models" by Coursera
- "AI Workflow: Enterprise Model Deployment" by IBM (Coursera)

Websites:

- AWS AI and Machine Learning (https://aws.amazon.com/machine-learning/)
- Microsoft Azure AI (https://azure.microsoft.com/en-us/services/machine-learning/)

Chapter 8: Ethical and Legal Considerations

Books:

- "Weapons of Math Destruction: How Big Data Increases Inequality and Threatens Democracy" by Cathy O'Neil
- "Ethics of Artificial Intelligence and Robotics" by Vincent C. Müller

Online Courses:

- "AI Ethics: Global Perspectives" by the University of Hong Kong (edX)
- "Ethics and Law in Data and Analytics" by the University of Michigan (Coursera)

Websites:

- AI Now Institute (https://ainowinstitute.org/)
- Future of Life Institute (https://futureoflife.org/)

Chapter 9: Managing Change

Books:

- "Leading Change" by John P. Kotter
- "The Change Management Handbook: A Road Map to Corporate Transformation" by David Miller and Philip Johnson

Online Courses:

- "Change Management" by the University of London (Coursera)
- "Leading Digital Transformation and Innovation" by INSEAD (Coursera)

Websites:

- Prosci Change Management (https://www.prosci.com/)
- Change Management Institute (https://www.change-management-institute.com/)

Chapter 10: Future Trends in AI
Books:

- "AI Superpowers: China, Silicon Valley, and the New World Order" by Kai-Fu Lee
- "The Fourth Industrial Revolution" by Klaus Schwab

Online Courses:

- "AI For Good" by the University of Auckland (FutureLearn)
- "The Future of AI" by MIT Professional Education

Websites:

- World Economic Forum on AI (https://www.weforum.org/agenda/archive/artificial-intelligence/)
- AI & Society Journal (https://www.springer.com/journal/146)

Conclusion

This comprehensive list of resources spans books, online courses, and websites, providing valuable insights and practical knowledge for each chapter of this book. These resources are designed to deepen your understanding of AI, from foundational concepts to advanced applications, and help you effectively implement AI in your business. Whether you are a business leader, manager, or AI practitioner, these resources will equip you with the tools and knowledge needed to navigate the AI landscape and drive successful AI initiatives.

APPENDICES

PROMPT - Describe in detail natural language processing

Natural Language Processing (NLP)

Introduction
Natural Language Processing (NLP) is a field of artificial intelligence that focuses on the interaction between computers and human (natural) languages. The goal of NLP is to enable machines to understand, interpret, and generate human language in a way that is both meaningful and useful. NLP encompasses a range of tasks, from basic language processing to complex text understanding and generation.

Key Components of NLP
Tokenization

- **Definition**: Tokenization is the process of breaking down a text into smaller units called tokens, which can be words, phrases, or even sentences.
- **Importance**: Tokenization is a crucial first step in text processing as it converts unstructured text into a structured format that can be analyzed.
- **Techniques**:
    - **Word Tokenization**: Splitting text into individual words.
    - **Sentence Tokenization**: Dividing text into sentences.
    - **Subword Tokenization**: Breaking down words into subwords or character-level tokens, useful for handling rare words.

Part-of-Speech Tagging (POS Tagging)

- **Definition**: POS tagging involves assigning parts of speech to each word in a sentence, such as nouns, verbs, adjectives, etc.
- **Importance**: Understanding the role of each word in a sentence helps in parsing and interpreting the text.
- **Techniques**:
    - **Rule-Based Tagging**: Using predefined grammatical rules to tag words.
    - **Statistical Tagging**: Employing probabilistic models like Hidden Markov Models (HMM) to predict POS tags.
    - **Neural Network Tagging**: Using deep learning models for more accurate tagging.

Named Entity Recognition (NER)

- **Definition**: NER identifies and classifies named entities in text, such as people, organizations, locations, dates, and other proper nouns.
- **Importance**: Extracting key entities from text is essential for information retrieval, data mining, and understanding context.
- **Techniques**:
    - **Dictionary-Based Methods**: Using predefined lists of entities.
    - **Rule-Based Methods**: Applying linguistic rules and patterns.
    - **Machine Learning Methods**: Training models on labeled datasets to recognize entities.

Sentiment Analysis

- **Definition**: Sentiment analysis determines the sentiment or emotion expressed in a piece of text, such as positive, negative, or neutral.
- **Importance**: Sentiment analysis is widely used in customer feedback analysis, social media monitoring, and market research.
- **Techniques**:
    - **Lexicon-Based Approaches**: Using dictionaries of words associated with specific sentiments.
    - **Machine Learning Approaches**: Training models to classify sentiments based on features extracted from text.
    - **Deep Learning Approaches**: Employing neural networks for more nuanced sentiment detection.

Text Classification

- **Definition**: Text classification involves categorizing text into predefined categories based on its content.
- **Importance**: Text classification is useful for organizing and managing large volumes of text data, such as emails, news articles, and documents.
- **Techniques**:
    - **Rule-Based Classification**: Using rules and patterns to classify text.
    - **Statistical Classification**: Applying probabilistic models like Naive Bayes.

- - **Machine Learning Classification**: Using algorithms like Support Vector Machines (SVM) and neural networks.

Machine Translation

- **Definition**: Machine translation automatically translates text from one language to another.
- **Importance**: Enables cross-language communication and access to information in multiple languages.
- **Techniques**:
  - **Rule-Based Translation**: Using linguistic rules and dictionaries.
  - **Statistical Machine Translation (SMT)**: Leveraging statistical models trained on bilingual text corpora.
  - **Neural Machine Translation (NMT)**: Using deep learning models for more accurate and fluent translations.

Language Generation

- **Definition**: Language generation involves producing coherent and contextually appropriate text from structured data or other inputs.
- **Importance**: Language generation is used in chatbots, content creation, and summarization.
- **Techniques**:
  - **Template-Based Generation**: Using predefined templates to generate text.

- Statistical Generation: Employing probabilistic models to generate text.
- Neural Network Generation: Using models like GPT-4 for sophisticated text generation.

NLP Applications
Chatbots and Virtual Assistants

- **Overview**: NLP-powered chatbots and virtual assistants interact with users through natural language, providing information, answering queries, and performing tasks.
- **Examples**: Siri, Alexa, Google Assistant.
- **Benefits**:
    - **24/7 Availability**: Provides round-the-clock assistance.
    - **Scalability**: Can handle a large volume of interactions simultaneously.
    - **Cost-Effective**: Reduces the need for human customer service agents.

Sentiment Analysis

- **Overview**: Sentiment analysis tools analyze text data to determine the sentiment expressed, helping businesses understand customer opinions and market trends.
- **Examples**: Analyzing social media posts, product reviews, and customer feedback.
- **Benefits**:
    - **Customer Insights**: Provides insights into customer satisfaction and preferences.

- o **Brand Monitoring**: Tracks brand reputation and public perception.
- o **Market Research**: Identifies trends and emerging issues in the market.

Text Summarization

- **Overview**: Text summarization algorithms condense long documents into shorter, coherent summaries while retaining key information.
- **Examples**: Summarizing news articles, research papers, and legal documents.
- **Benefits**:
  - o **Time-Saving**: Helps users quickly grasp the main points of long texts.
  - o **Information Overload**: Manages large volumes of information efficiently.
  - o **Accessibility**: Makes content more accessible by providing concise summaries.

Language Translation

- **Overview**: Machine translation systems translate text from one language to another, enabling cross-language communication and information access.
- **Examples**: Google Translate, Microsoft Translator.
- **Benefits**:
  - o **Global Reach**: Breaks down language barriers, allowing businesses to reach international audiences.

- o **Information Access**: Provides access to content in multiple languages.
- o **Cost-Effective**: Reduces the need for human translators.

Information Retrieval

- **Overview**: Information retrieval systems use NLP to search and retrieve relevant information from large text corpora or databases.
- **Examples**: Search engines, digital libraries, and knowledge management systems.
- **Benefits**:
  - o **Efficiency**: Quickly finds relevant information from vast datasets.
  - o **Accuracy**: Improves search accuracy with contextual understanding.
  - o **Usability**: Enhances user experience with natural language queries.

NLP Challenges and Future Directions
Challenges

- **Ambiguity**: Human language is often ambiguous, with words and phrases having multiple meanings depending on context.
- **Context Understanding**: Grasping the context and nuances of language remains difficult for machines.
- **Data Privacy**: Handling sensitive information in text data while ensuring privacy and security.

- **Bias and Fairness**: Addressing biases in training data to ensure fair and unbiased NLP models.
- **Language Diversity**: Developing models that can handle multiple languages and dialects effectively.

Future Directions

- **Improved Contextual Understanding**: Advancements in deep learning and contextual embeddings (e.g., BERT, GPT-3) are enhancing machines' ability to understand context.
- **Multimodal NLP**: Integrating text with other modalities like images and audio for richer understanding and interaction.
- **Ethical NLP**: Developing frameworks and guidelines to address ethical concerns and biases in NLP models.
- **Low-Resource Languages**: Focusing on improving NLP capabilities for low-resource and underrepresented languages.
- **Real-Time Processing**: Enhancing the speed and efficiency of NLP systems to enable real-time applications.

Conclusion

Natural Language Processing is a dynamic and rapidly evolving field with vast potential across various industries. By enabling machines to understand and interact with human language, NLP opens up new possibilities for automation, customer engagement, and data-driven insights. Despite the challenges, ongoing advancements in AI and machine learning are continuously improving the capabilities and applications of NLP, making it an essential component of modern AI solutions.

PROMPT - Provide a framework for analyzing AI case studies, including key questions to consider and metric uses to evaluate

Framework for Analyzing AI Case Studies

Analyzing AI case studies involves understanding the context, implementation, outcomes, and lessons learned from AI projects. This framework provides a structured approach to analyzing AI case studies, helping readers extract valuable insights and apply them to their own initiatives.

Key Components of the Framework
1. **Background and Context**
    - **Industry and Organization**: Identify the industry and specific organization involved in the case study.
    - **Business Problem**: Define the business problem or opportunity that the AI solution aims to address.
    - **Objectives**: Clarify the objectives and goals of the AI project.
2. **Data Collection and Preparation**
    - **Data Sources**: Determine the sources of data used in the AI project (e.g., historical records, sensor data, customer interactions).
    - **Data Quality**: Assess the quality and completeness of the data.
    - **Data Processing**: Evaluate the methods used for data cleaning, transformation, and preparation.
3. **AI Model Development and Implementation**
    - **Model Selection**: Identify the type of AI models used (e.g., machine learning, deep learning, NLP).

- **Development Process**: Describe the development process, including model training, validation, and testing.
- **Integration**: Explain how the AI models were integrated into existing systems and workflows.

4. **Outcomes and Impact**
    - **Performance Metrics**: Evaluate the performance of the AI models using relevant metrics (e.g., accuracy, precision, recall).
    - **Business Impact**: Measure the impact of the AI solution on key business metrics (e.g., cost savings, revenue growth, efficiency improvements).
    - **User Feedback**: Gather feedback from users and stakeholders on the effectiveness and usability of the AI solution.
5. **Challenges and Lessons Learned**
    - **Technical Challenges**: Identify technical challenges encountered during the project (e.g., data issues, model limitations).
    - **Organizational Challenges**: Describe organizational challenges (e.g., resistance to change, resource allocation).
    - **Lessons Learned**: Summarize the lessons learned and best practices for future AI projects.

Key Questions to Consider
1. **Background and Context**
    - What industry and organization are involved in the case study?
    - What specific business problem or opportunity is being addressed?
    - What are the primary objectives and goals of the AI project?
2. **Data Collection and Preparation**
    - What data sources were used for the AI project?
    - How was the quality and completeness of the data ensured?
    - What methods were used for data cleaning and preparation?
3. **AI Model Development and Implementation**
    - What types of AI models were selected and why?
    - What was the process for developing, validating, and testing the models?
    - How were the models integrated into existing systems and workflows?
4. **Outcomes and Impact**
    - What performance metrics were used to evaluate the AI models?
    - How did the AI solution impact key business metrics?
    - What feedback did users and stakeholders provide on the AI solution?
5. **Challenges and Lessons Learned**
    - What technical challenges were encountered during the project?
    - What organizational challenges were faced?

- o What lessons were learned, and what best practices emerged?

Metrics to Evaluate
1. **Performance Metrics**
    - o **Accuracy**: The proportion of correct predictions made by the AI model.
    - o **Precision**: The proportion of true positive predictions out of all positive predictions.
    - o **Recall (Sensitivity)**: The proportion of true positive predictions out of all actual positives.
    - o **F1 Score**: The harmonic mean of precision and recall, providing a balanced measure.
    - o **ROC-AUC**: The area under the receiver operating characteristic curve, indicating the model's ability to distinguish between classes.
2. **Business Impact Metrics**
    - o **Cost Savings**: The reduction in costs resulting from the AI solution.
    - o **Revenue Growth**: The increase in revenue attributable to the AI solution.
    - o **Efficiency Improvements**: The improvements in operational efficiency (e.g., time savings, process optimization).
    - o **Customer Satisfaction**: The improvement in customer satisfaction metrics (e.g., Net Promoter Score, customer feedback).
3. **User Feedback Metrics**
    - o **User Adoption**: The rate at which users adopt and use the AI solution.

- **Usability**: User feedback on the ease of use and intuitiveness of the AI solution.
- **Satisfaction**: Overall satisfaction of users and stakeholders with the AI solution.

By applying this framework to analyze AI case studies, organizations can gain a deeper understanding of the critical factors that contribute to successful AI implementations, identify potential challenges, and adopt best practices for their own AI projects.

PROMPT - Provide templates for documenting AI projects and capturing lessons learned

Templates for Documenting AI Projects and Capturing Lessons Learned

To effectively document AI projects and capture lessons learned, the following templates can be used. These templates help ensure comprehensive documentation, facilitate knowledge sharing, and promote continuous improvement.

Template 1: AI Project Documentation
Project Overview

- **Project Title**: [Enter Project Title]
- **Project Manager**: [Enter Project Manager Name]
- **Team Members**: [Enter Team Members]
- **Start Date**: [Enter Start Date]
- **End Date**: [Enter End Date]
- **Status**: [Enter Status (e.g., Ongoing, Completed)]

Background and Objectives

- **Industry and Organization**: [Describe the industry and organization]
- **Business Problem/Opportunity**: [Describe the business problem or opportunity]
- **Objectives**: [List the primary objectives and goals of the AI project]

Data Collection and Preparation

- **Data Sources**: [List the data sources used]
- **Data Quality**: [Describe data quality and completeness]
- **Data Processing**: [Describe methods for data cleaning and preparation]

AI Model Development

- **Model Selection**: [Describe the AI models used]
- **Development Process**: [Detail the model training, validation, and testing process]
- **Tools and Technologies**: [List the tools and technologies used]

Implementation

- **Integration**: [Describe how models were integrated into systems and workflows]
- **Deployment**: [Detail the deployment process and environment]

Outcomes and Impact

- **Performance Metrics**: [List performance metrics and results]
- **Business Impact**: [Describe the impact on key business metrics]
- **User Feedback**: [Summarize user and stakeholder feedback]

Challenges and Solutions

- **Technical Challenges**: [List technical challenges encountered and solutions]
- **Organizational Challenges**: [List organizational challenges and solutions]

Lessons Learned

- **Success Factors**: [Identify key success factors]
- **Areas for Improvement**: [Highlight areas for improvement]
- **Best Practices**: [List best practices for future projects]

Appendix

- **References**: [List references and resources used]
- **Additional Documentation**: [Attach additional documentation if needed]

Template 2: Lessons Learned Documentation
Project Title: [Enter Project Title]
Date: [Enter Date]
Team Members: [Enter Team Members]
Lessons Learned Summary
1. What Went Well

- **Success Factors**: [Describe what went well and why]
    - Example: "The data quality was high, which enabled accurate model predictions."
- **Best Practices**: [Identify best practices that contributed to success]
    - Example: "Regular communication between data scientists and clinicians ensured model relevance."

2. Challenges and Solutions

- **Technical Challenges**: [Describe technical challenges and solutions]
    - Example: "Data integration was challenging due to different formats. Solution: Developed a standardized data preprocessing pipeline."
- **Organizational Challenges**: [Describe organizational challenges and solutions]
    - Example: "Resistance to change among staff. Solution: Conducted training sessions to demonstrate the AI benefits."

3. Areas for Improvement

- **Improvements Needed**: [Highlight areas that need improvement]
    - Example: "Need for more diverse training data to improve model generalizability."
- **Recommendations**: [Provide recommendations for future projects]
    - Example: "Implement a more rigorous data validation process early in the project."

4. Impact on Future Projects

- **Adjustments to Processes**: [Describe how the lessons learned will impact future projects]
    - Example: "Incorporate a phased rollout plan to gradually introduce AI solutions and gather feedback."

5. Additional Comments

- [Include any additional comments or insights]

Example: Filled Template for an AI Project
Project Overview

- **Project Title**: Predictive Maintenance for Manufacturing Equipment
- **Project Manager**: John Doe
- **Team Members**: Jane Smith, Michael Brown, Sarah Johnson
- **Start Date**: January 1, 2023
- **End Date**: December 31, 2023
- **Status**: Completed

Background and Objectives

- **Industry and Organization**: Manufacturing, XYZ Corp
- **Business Problem/Opportunity**: High unplanned downtime due to equipment failures
- **Objectives**: Reduce downtime by 20%, lower maintenance costs, and improve equipment reliability

Data Collection and Preparation

- **Data Sources**: Sensor data from equipment, maintenance logs
- **Data Quality**: Ensured completeness and accuracy of sensor data
- **Data Processing**: Standardized data preprocessing and cleaning pipeline

AI Model Development

- **Model Selection**: Random Forest, LSTM for time-series analysis
- **Development Process**: Trained on historical data, validated using cross-validation, tested on unseen data
- **Tools and Technologies**: Python, TensorFlow, Sklearn, AWS SageMaker

Implementation

- **Integration**: Integrated with existing maintenance management system
- **Deployment**: Deployed on cloud infrastructure for scalability

Outcomes and Impact

- **Performance Metrics**: Model accuracy: 85%, Precision: 80%, Recall: 78%
- **Business Impact**: Reduced downtime by 25%, saved $500,000 in maintenance costs
- **User Feedback**: Positive feedback from maintenance team, improved efficiency

Challenges and Solutions

- **Technical Challenges**: Initial data integration issues solved by creating a unified data format
- **Organizational Challenges**: Addressed resistance through training and demonstration of benefits

Lessons Learned

- **Success Factors**: High-quality data, close collaboration with maintenance team
- **Areas for Improvement**: Need for more diverse data to cover all failure modes
- **Best Practices**: Regularly update models with new data, involve end-users in the development process

Appendix

- **References**: Internal documentation, academic papers on predictive maintenance
- **Additional Documentation**: Detailed model development and validation reports

---

By using these templates, organizations can ensure thorough documentation of AI projects and systematically capture valuable lessons learned, promoting continuous improvement and knowledge sharing across teams.

---

www.ingramcontent.com/pod-product-compliance
Lightning Source LLC
Chambersburg PA
CBHW071920210526
45479CB00002B/486